Hannah More

Sacred Dramas

Chiefly Intended for Young Persons

Hannah More

Sacred Dramas
Chiefly Intended for Young Persons

ISBN/EAN: 9783744712644

Printed in Europe, USA, Canada, Australia, Japan

Cover: Foto ©ninafisch / pixelio.de

More available books at **www.hansebooks.com**

SACRED DRAMAS,

CHIEFLY INTENDED

For YOUNG PERSONS:

THE SUBJECTS TAKEN FROM THE BIBLE.

To which are added :

REFLECTIONS OF KING HEZEKIAH,

A N D

SENSIBILITY,

A POEM.

By HANNAH MORE.

All the Books of the BIBLE are either moſt admirable
and exalted Pieces of Poetry, or are the beſt materials in
the world for it.   COWLEY.

PHILADELPHIA:

PRINTED FOR THOMAS DOBSON, IN SECOND-STREET,
BETWEEN MARKET AND CHESNUT-STREET.
M,DCC,LXXXVII.

TO HER GRACE

THE DUCHESS OF BEAUFORT;

THESE SACRED DRAMAS

ARE, WITH THE MOST PERFECT RESPECT,

INSCRIBED:

AS, AMONG THE MANY AMIABLE

AND DISTINGUISHED QUALIT

WHICH ADORN HER MIND,

AND ADD LUSTRE TO HER RA

ER EXCELLENCE IN THE MATERNAL

GIVES A PECULIAR PROPRIE

TO HER PROTECTION OF THIS LITTL

WRITTEN WITH AN HUMBLE W

TO PROMOTE THE LOVE OF PIETY A

IN YOUNG PERSONS;

BY HER GRACE'S

MOST OBEDIENT,

MOST OBLIGED, AND

MOST HUMBLE SERVANT,

H. MORE.

A 2

ADVERTISEMENT.

I AM as ready as the moſt rigid Critic, to confeſs, that nothing can be more ſimple and inartificial than the plans of the following Dramas. In the conſtruction of them, I have ſeldom ventured to introduce any perſons * of my own creation: ſtill leſs did I imagine myſelf at liberty to invent circumſtances. I reflected, with awe, *that the place where-on I ſtood was holy ground.* All the latitude I permitted my-ſelf, was, to make ſuch perſons as I ſelected, act under ſuch circumſtances as I found; and expreſs ſuch ſentiments as, in my humble judgment, appeared not unnatural to their ſituations.—Some of the ſpeeches are ſo long as to retard the action; for I rather aſpired after Moral Inſtruc-tion, than the purity of Dramatic Compoſition. The very terms of Act and Scene are avoided; becauſe I was un-willing

---

* *Never, indeed, except in* DANIEL, *and that of neceſ-ſity; as the Bible furniſhes no more than two perſons, Da-niel and Darius; and theſe were not ſufficient to carry on the buſineſs of the Piece.*

willing to awaken the attention of the Reader to my defi-
ciencies in critical exactnefs.

It will be thought that I have chofen, perhaps, the
leaft important paffage in the eventful Life of David, for
the foundation of the Drama which bears his name. Yet
even in this, his firft exploit, the facced Hiftorian repre-
fents him as exhibiting no mean leffon of modefty, humi-
lity, courage, and piety ; virtues not only admirable, but
imitable ; and within the reach of every Reader. Many
will think, that the introduction of Saul's daughter would
have added to the effect of the piece : and I have no
doubt, but that it would have made the intrigue more
complicated, and more interefting, had this Drama been
intended for the Stage. There, all that is tender, and all
that is terrible in the paffions, find a proper place. But I
write for the Young, in whom it will be always time
enough to have them awakened ; I write for a clafs of
Readers, to whom it is not eafy to accommodate one fub-
ject *.

A very judicious and learned friend has remarked, that
the *Reflections of King Hezekiah* breathe rather too much
of

---

* *It would not be eafy, I believe, to introduce Sacred
Tragedies on the Englifh Stage. The fcrupulous would
think it profane, while the profane would think it dull.
Yet the excellent* RACINE, *in a diffipated country, and a
voluptuous court, ventured to adapt the ftory of* Athaliah *to
the French Theatre ; and it remains to us a glorious monu-
ment of its Author's courageous piety, and of the perfection
of the Dramatic Art.*

of the fpirit of Chriftianity; for that it is fcarcely probable he had fo fettled a belief in the General Judgment. I feel the juftnefs of the objection, without having been able to obviate it. I wifhed to convey a ftrong idea of this great leading truth; and have, perhaps improperly, afcribed fentiments to a Jewifh monarch, merely becaufe I wifhed to imprefs them on the Chriftian Reader.

The Critic and the Scholar, if any fuch fhould honour thefe pages with their attention, will find ample matter on which to exercife their candor and charity; qualities fo natural to genius and to learning, that even the feeblenefs of my performance will not be able to obftruct the exertion of them in favour of my intention.

The amiable Poet * from whom I have taken my motto, after fhewing the fuperiority of the Sacred, over the Profane Hiftories (fome inftances of which I have noticed in my Introduction), concludes with the following remark, which I may apply to myfelf with more propriety than it was ufed by the Author :—" I am far from " affuming to myfelf, to have fulfilled the duty of this " weighty undertaking; and I fhall be ambitious of no o- " ther fruit from this weak and imperfect attempt of " mine, but the opening of a way to the courage and in- " duftry of fome other perfons, who may be better able " to perform it thoroughly and fuccefsfully."

---

* *Cowley.*

THE

INTRODUCTION.

O FOR the facred energy, which ftruck
The harp of Jeffe's fon ! or for a fpark
Of that celeftial flame, which touch'd the lips
Of blefs'd Ifaiah* ; when the Seraphim
With living fire defcended, and his foul
From fin's pollution purg'd ! or one faint ray,
(If human things to heavenly I may join)
Of that pure fpirit, which inflam'd the breaft
Of Milton, GOD's own poet ! when, retir'd,
In fair enthufiaftic vifion rapt,
The *nightly vifitant* deign'd blefs his couch
With infpiration, fuch as never flow'd
From Aganippe's fount, or Acidale !
Then, when the facred fire within him burnt,
He fpake, as man or angel might have fpoke,
When man was pure, and angels were his guefts.

That

---

* *Ifaiah, chap.* vi.

It will not be.—Nor prophet's burning zeal,
Nor mufe of fire, nor yet to fweep the ftrings
With facred energy to me belongs;
Nor with Miltonic hand to touch the chords,
That wake to ecftacy.   From me, alas!
The fecret fource of harmony is hid;
The magic powers which catch the ravifh'd foul
In melody's fweet maze, and the clear ftreams
Which to pure Fancy's yet untafted fprings
Enchanted lead.   Of thefe I nothing know;
Yet, all unknowing, dare thy aid invoke,
Spirit of Truth! who gracioufly haft faid,
That none who afk in faith fhould afk in vain,

You I invoke not now, ye fabled Nine!
I not invoke you, though you well were fought
In Greece and Latium, by immortal bards,
Whofe fyren fong enchants; and fhall enchant,
Thro' Time's wide-circling round, tho' falfe their faith,
And lefs than human were the gods they fung.
'Tho' falfe their faith, they taught the beft they knew;
And, blufh, O Chriftians! liv'd above their faith.
They wou'd have blefs'd the beam, and hail'd the day,
Which chafs'd the moral darknefs from their fouls.
Oh! had their minds receiv'd the clearer ray
Of true devotion; they had learn'd to fcorn
Their deities impure, their fenfelefs gods,
And wild mythology's fantaftic maze.

Pure PLATO! how had thy chafte fpirit hail'd
A faith fo fitted to thy moral fenfe!
What had'ft thou felt, to fee the fair romance
Of high imagination, the bright dream

Of

Of thy pure fancy more than realiz'd!
O sweet enthusiast! thou hadst blest a scheme
Fair, good, and perfect. How had thy rapt soul
Caught fire, and burnt with a diviner flame!
For ev'n thy fair idea ne'er conceiv'd
Such plenitude of love, such boundless bliss,
As Deity made visible to sense.
Unhappy BRUTUS! philosophic mind!
Great 'midst the errors of the Stoic school!
How had his kindling spirit joy'd to find
That his lov'd virtue was no empty name:
Nor had he met the vision at Philippi;
Nor had he sheath'd his bloody dagger's point,
Or in the breast he lov'd, or in his own.

The Pagan page how far more wise than ours!
They with the gods they worship'd grac'd their song;
Our song was grace with gods we disbelieve;
The manners we adopt without the creed.
Shall Fiction only raise poetic flame,
And shall no altars blaze, O TRUTH! to thee?
Shall falsehood only please, and fable charm?
And shall eternal Truth neglected lie?
Because immortal, slighted or profan'd?
Truth has our rev'rence only, not our love;
Our praise, but not our heart. A deity,
Confess'd, but shunn'd; acknowledg'd, not ador'd;
She comes too near us, and she shines too bright'
Her penetrating beam at once betrays
What we would hide from others and ourselves.

Why shun to make our duty our delight?
Let *pleasure* be the motive (and allow

That

That immortality be quite forgot :)
Where fhall we trace, thro' all the page profane,
A livelier pleafure, and a purer fource
Of innocent delight, than the fair book
Of holy Truth prefents ? For ardent youth,
The fprightly narrative ; for years mature,
The moral document, in fober robe
Of grave philofophy array'd : which all
Had heard with admiration, had embrac'd
With rapture ; had the fhades of Academe,
Or the learn'd Porch produc'd it.   Then, O then,
How Wifdom's hidden treafures had been couch'd
Beneath fair Allegory's graceful veil !

Do not the pow'rs of foul-enchanting fong,
Strong imag'ry, bold figure, every charm
Of eaftern fiight fublime, apt metaphor,
And all the graces in thy lovely train,
Divine Simplicity ! affemble all
In Sion's fongs, and bold Ifaiah's ftrain ?

Why fhou'd the claffic eye delight to trace
How Pyrrha and the fam'd Theffalian * king
Reftor'd the ruin'd race of loft mankind ;
Yet turn, incurious, from the patriarch fav'd;
The righteous remnant of a delug'd world ?
Why are we taught, delighted, to recount
Alcides' labours, yet negleft to learn
How migthy Samfon led a life of toil
Herculean ? Pain and peril mark'd them both ;

A life

---

* _Deucalion._

A life eventful, and difaftrous death.
Can all the tales, which Grecian records yield ;
Can all the names the Roman page records,
Renown'd for friendfhip and furpaffing love ;
Can gallant Thefeus and his brave compeer ; •
Oreftes, and the partner of his toils ;
Achates and his friend ; Euryalus,
And blooming Nifus, pleafant in their lives,
And undivided by the ftroke of death ;
Can each, can all, a lovelier picture yield
Of virtuous friendfhip : can they all prefent
A tendernefs more touching than the love
Of Jonathan and David ?—Speak, ye young!
You who are undebauch'd by fafhion's lore,
And, unfophifticate, from nature judge,
Say, is your quick attention ftronger drawn,
By wafted Thebes, than Pharaoh's fmitten hofts ?
Or do the vagrant Trojans yield a theme
More grateful to the eager appetite
Of young impatience, than the wand'ring tribes,
By Mofes thro' the thirfty defert led?
The beauteous * Maid (tho' tender is the tale),
Whofe guiltlefs blood on Aulis' altar ftream'd,
Smites not the bofom with a fofter pang
Than Jephthah's daughter, doom'd like her to die.

Such are the lovely themes, which court the Mufe,
Scarce yet effay'd in verfe. O let me mourn,
That heav'n-defcended fong fhould e'er forget
Its facred dignity, and high defcent;
Should e'er fo far its origin debafe,

To

---

* *Iphigenia.*

To fpread corruption's bane, to lull the bad
With flattery's opiate ftrain ; to taint the heart
Of innocence, and filently infufe
Delicious poifon, whofe infidious charm
Feeds the fick mind, and fondly minifters
Unwholfome pleafure to the fever'd tafte ;
While its fell venom, with malignant pow'r,
Strikes at the root of virtue, with'ring all
Her vital energy. Oh ! for fome balm
Of fov'reign power, to raife the drooping Mufe
To all the health of virtue ! to infufe
A gen'rous warmth, to roufe an holy pride,
And give her high conceptions of herfelf !

    For me, eternal Spirit ! let thy word
My path illume ! O thou compaffionate GOD !
Thou know'ft our frame, thou know'ft we are but duft:
From duft a Seraph's zeal thou wilt not afk,
An Angel's purity. Oh ! as I ftrive,
Tho' with a feeble voice and flagging wing,
A glowing heart, but pow'rlefs hand, to tell
The faith of favour'd man to heav'n, to fing
The ways infcrutable of heav'n to man ;
May I, by thy celeftial guidance led,
Fix deeper in my heart the truths I fing !
In my own life tranfcribe whate'er of good
To others I propofe ! and by thy rule
Correct th' irregular *, reform the wrong,

                                Exalt

---

        * *What in me is dark*
Illumine, what is low raife and fupport.
                        PARADISE LOST.

Exalt the low, and brighten the obſcure !
Still may I note, how all th' agreeing parts
Of this well-order'd fabric join to frame
One fair, one finiſh'd, one harmonious whole !
Trace the cloſe links, which form the perfect chain
In beautiful connection ; mark the ſcale,
Whoſe nice gradations, with progreſſion true,
For ever riſing, end in DEITY !

PER-

PERSONS of the DRAMA.

HEBREW WOMEN.

JOCHEBED, Mother of Moses.
MIRIAM, his Sister.

EGYPTIANS.

The PRINCESS, King PHARAOH's Daughter; MELI-
TA; and other Attendants.

SCENE on the Banks of the NILE.

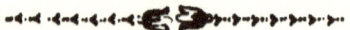

☞ The Subject is taken from the Second Chapter of
the Book of Exodus.

MOSES IN THE BULRUSHES:

A

SACRED DRAMA.

PART I.

'I will affert eternal Providence,
And juftify the ways of God to man.
PERADISE LOST.

JOCHEBED, MIRIAM.

JOCHEBED.

WHY was my pray'r accepted ? why did heav'n
In anger hear me, when I afk'd a fon ?
Ye dames of Egypt ! happy, happy mothers !
No tyrant robs you of your fondeft hopes ;
You are not doom'd to fee the babes you bore,
The babes you nurture, bleed before your eyes !
You tafte the tranfports of maternal love,
And never know its anguifh ! happy mothers !

C

How

How diff'rent is the lot of thy fad daughters,
O wretched Ifrael! Was it then for this?
Was it for this the righteous arm of GOD
Refcued his chofen people from the jaws
Of cruel want, by pious Jofeph's care?
Jofeph! th' elected inftrument of heav'n,
Decreed to fave illuftrious Abraham's race,
What time the famine rag'd in Canaan's land.
Ifrael, who then was fpar'd, muft perifh now!

Oh thou myfterious pow'r! who haft involv'd
Thy wife decrees in darknefs, to perplex
The pride of human wifdom, to confound
The daring fcrutiny, and prove the faith
Of thy prefuming creatures! clear this doubt;
Teach me to trace this maze of Providence;
Why fave the fathers, if the fons muft perifh?

MIRIAM.
Ah me, my mother! whence thefe floods of grief?

JOCHEBED.
My fon! my fon! I cannot fpeak the reft.
Ye who have fons can only know my fondnefs!
Ye who have loft them, or who fear to lofe,
Can only know my pangs! none elfe can guefs them.
A mother's forrows cannot be conceiv'd,
But by a mother—Wherefore am I one?

MIRIAM.
With many pray'rs thou didft requeft this fon,
And heav'n has granted him.

JOCHEBED.

JOCHEBED.

O fad eftate
Of human wretchednefs! fo weak is man,
So ignorant and blind, that did not GOD
Sometimes withhold in mercy what we afk,
We fhou'd be ruin'd at our own requeft.

Too well thou know'ft, my child, the ftern decree
Of Egypt's cruel king, hard-hearted Pharaoh;
" That ev'ry male, of Hebrew mother born,
" Muft die." Oh! do I live to tell it thee?
Muft die a bloody death! My child, my fon,
My youngeft born, my darling muft be flain!

MIRIAM.

The helplefs innocent! and muft he die?

JOCHEBED.

No: if a mother's tears, a mother's pray'rs,
A mother's fond precautions can prevail,
He fhall not die. I have a thought, my Miriam!
And fure the GOD of mercies, who infpir'd,
Will blefs the fecret purpofe of my foul,
To fave his precious life.

MIRIAM.

Hop'ft thou that Pharaoh—

JOCHEBED.

I have no hope in Pharaoh, much in GOD;
Much in the ROCK OF AGES.

C 2 MIRIAM.

MIRIAM.
Think, O think,
What perils thou already haft incur'd ;
And fhun the greater, which may yet remain.
Three months,'three dang'rous months thou haft preferv'd
Thy infant's life, and in thy houfe conceal'd him!
Shou'd Pharaoh know !

JOCHEBED.
Oh! let the tyrant know,
And feel what he inflicts! Yes, hear me, Heav'n!
Send the right aiming thunderbolts——But hufh,
My impious murmurs ! Is it not thy will ;
Thou, infinite in mercy ? Thou permitt'ft
This feeming evil for fome latent good.
Yes, I will laud thy grace, and blefs thy goodnefs,
For what I have, and not arraign thy wifdom
For what I fear to lofe. O, I will blefs thee,
That Aaron will be fpar'd! that my firft-born
Lives fafe and undifturb'd ! that he was given me-
Before this impious perfecution rag'd !

MIRIAM.
And yet who knows, but the fell tyrant's rage
May reach *his* precious life ?

JOCHEBED.
I fear for him,.
For thee, for all. A doating parent lives
In many lives ; thro' many a nerve fhe feels ;
From child to child the quick affections fpread,
For ever wand'ring, yet for ever fix'd.

Nor does divifion weaken, nor the force
Of conftant operation e'er exhauft
Parental love. All other paffions change,
With changing circumftances ; rife or fall,
Dependant on their object ; claim returns ;
Live on reciprocation, and expire
Unfed by hope. A mother's fondnefs reigns
Without a rival, and without an end.

MIRIAM.

But fay what Heav'n infpires, to fave thy fon ?

JOCHEBED.

Since the dear fatal morn which gave him birth,
I have revolv'd in my diftracted mind
Each means to fave his life : and many a thought,
Which fondnefs prompted, prudence has oppos'd
As perilous and rafh. With thefe poor hands
I've fram'd a little ark of flender reeds ;
With pitch and flime I have fecur'd the fides.
In this frail cradle I intend to lay
My little helplefs infant, and expofe him
Upon the banks of Nile.

MIRIAM.
'Tis full of danger.

JOCHEBED.
'Tis danger to expofe, and death to keep him.

MIRIAM.
Yet, Oh! reflect. Shou'd the fierce crocodile.
The native and the tyrant of the NILE.
Seize the defencelefs infant !

JOCHEBED.

JOCHEBED.
Oh, forbear!
Spare my fond heart. Yet not the crocodile,
Nor all the deadly monſters of the deep,
To me are half ſo terrible as PHARAOH,
That heathen king, that royal murderer!

MIRIAM.
Shou'd he eſcape, which yet I dare not hope,
Each ſea-born monſter; yet the winds and waves
He cannot 'ſcape.

JOCHEBED.
Know, GOD is ev'ry where;
Not to one narrow, partial ſpot confin'd;
No, not to choſen ISRAEL: He extends
Thro' all the vaſt infinitude of ſpace.
At his command the furious tempeſts riſe,
The blaſting of the breath of his diſpleaſure:
He tells the world of waters, when to roar;
And at his bidding, winds and ſeas are calm.
In HIM, not in an arm of fleſh, I truſt;
In HIM, whoſe promiſe never yet has fail'd,
I place my confidence.

MIRIAM.
What muſt I do?
Command thy daughter, for thy words have wak'd
An holy boldneſs in my youthful breaſt.

JOCHEBED.
Go then, my MIRIAM! go, and take the infant
Buried in harmleſs ſlumbers there he lies:

Let

Let me not ſee him—ſpare my heart that pang.
Yet ſure, one little look may be indulg'd,
One kiſs—perhaps the laſt. No more, my ſoul!
That fondneſs wou'd be fatal——I ſhou'd keep him.
I cou'd not doom to death the babe I claſp'd:
Did ever mother kill her ſleeping boy?
I dare not hazard it——The taſk be thine.
Oh! do not wake my child; remove him ſoftly;
And gently lay him on the river's brink.

MIRIAM.

Did thoſe magicians, whom the ſons of EGYPT
Conſult, and think all-potent, join their ſkill,
And was it great as EGYPT's ſons believe;
Yet all their ſecret wizard arts combin'd,
To ſave this little ark of Bulruſhes,
Thus fearfully expos'd, cou'd not effect it.
Their ſpells, their incantations, and dire charms
Cou'd not preſerve it.

JOCHEBED.

              Know, this ark is charm'd
With ſpells, which impious EGYPT never knew;
With invocations to the living GOD,
I twiſted every ſlender reed together,
And with a pray'r did every ozier weave.

MIRIAM.

I go.

JOCHEBED.

Yet e'er thou go'ſt, obſerve me well.
When thou haſt laid him in his watry bed,

                  O leave

O leave him not; but at a diftance wait,
And mark what Heav'n's high will determines for him.
Lay him among the flags on yonder beach,
Juft where the royal gardens meet the Nile.
I dare not follow him, Sufpicion's eye
Wou'd note my wild demeanor; MIRIAM, yes,
The mother's fondnefs wou'd betray the child.
Farewell! GOD of my fathers, Oh protect him!

MOSES IN THE BULRUSHES.

PART II.

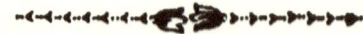

SCENE, on the Banks of the NILE.

Enter MIRIAM, *after having depofited the child.*

YES, I have laid him in his watry bed,
His watry grave, I fear!——I tremble ftill;
It was a cruel tafk——ftill I muft weep!
But ah! my mother, who fhall footh thy griefs?
The flags and fea-weeds will awhile fuftain
Their precious load, but it muft fink ere long!
Sweet babe, farewell! Yet think not I will leave thee;
No, I will watch thee, till the greedy waves

Devour

Devour thy little bark: I'll fit me down,
And fing to thee, fweet babe! Thou can'ft not hear;
But 'twill amufe me, while I watch thy fate.

       [Sbe fits down on a bank, and fings.

S O N G.

I.

THOU, who canft make the feeble ftrong,
  O GOD of Ifrael, hear my fong!
Not mine fuch notes as Egypt's daughters raife;
'Tis thee, O GOD of Hofts, I ftrive to praife.

II.

Ye winds, the fervants of the LORD,
Ye waves, obedient to his word,
O fpare the babe committed to your truft;
And Ifrael fhall confefs, the LORD is juft!

III.

Tho' doom'd to find an early grave,
This helplefs infant thou canft fave;
And he, whofe death's decreed by Pharaoh's hand,
May rife a prophet to redeem the land.

       [Sbe rifes, and looks out.

D   Who

Who moves this way ? of royal port she seems ;
Perhaps sent hither by the hand of Heav'n,
To prop the falling house of Levi.————Soft !
I'll listen unperceiv'd, these trees will hide me.

[*She stands behind.*

Enter the PRINCESS *of* EGYPT, *attended by a train
of Ladies.*

PRINCESS.

No farther, Virgins ; here I mean to rest,
To taste the pleasant coolness of the breeze ;
Perhaps to bathe in this translucent stream.
Did not our holy law * enjoin th' ablution
Frequent and regular ; it still were needful,
To mitigate the fervors of our clime.
MELITA, stay—the rest at distance wait.

[*They all go out, except one.*

The PRINCESS *looks out.*
Sure, or I much mistake, or I perceive,
Upon the sedgy margin of the Nile
A chest ; entangled in the reeds it seems ;
Discern'st thou ought ?

MELITA.
Something, but what I know not.

PRINCESS.

---

* *The ancient Egyptians used to wash their bodies four
times every twenty-four hours.*

PRINCESS.

Go and examine, what this fight may mean.

[*Exit Maid.*

MIRIAM, *behind.*

O bleft, beyond my hopes! he is difcover'd;
My brother will be fav'd! who is this ftranger?
Ah! 'tis the Princefs, cruel Pharaoh's daughter.
If fhe refemble her inhuman Sire,
She muft be cruel too; yet fame reports her
Moft merciful and mild:—I'll mark th' event,
And pray that Heav'n may prompt her to preferve him.

Re-enter MELITA.

PRINCESS.

Haft thou difcover'd what the veffel is?

MELITA.

Oh, Princefs, I have feen the ftrangeft fight!
Within the veffel lies a fleeping babe,
A fairer infant have I never feen!

PRINCESS.

Who knows, but fome unhappy Hebrew woman
Has thus expos'd her infant, to evade
The ftern decree of my too cruel Sire.
Unhappy mothers! oft my heart has bled
In fecret anguifh o'er your flaughter'd fons.

MELITA.

Shou'd this be one, my Princefs knows the danger.

D 2   PRINCESS.

PRINCESS.

No danger fhou'd deter from acts of mercy.

MIRIAM, *behind.*

A thoufand bleflings on her princely head !

PRINCESS.

Too much the fons of Jacob have endur'd
From royal Pharaoh's unrelenting hate ;
Too much our houfe has crufh'd their alien race.
Is't not enough, that cruel tafk-mafters
Grind them by hard oppreflion and ftern bondage ?
Is't not enough, my father owes his greatnefs,
His palaces, his fanes magnificent;
Thofe ftructures which the world with wonder views,
To the hard toils of much infulted Ifrael ?
To them his growing cities owe their fplendor,
Their labours built fair Ramefes and Pythom ;
And now, at length, his ftill increafing rage
To iron bondage adds the guilt of murder.
And fhall this little helplefs infant perifh ?
Forbid it, juftice ; and forbid it, heav'n !

MELITA.

I know, thy royal father fears the ftrength
Of this ftill growing race, who flourifh more
The more they are opprefs'd ; he dreads their numbers.

PRINCESS.

Apis forbid ! Pharaoh afraid of Ifrael !
Yet fhou'd this outcaft race, this haplefs people
E'er grow to fuch a formidable greatnefs :

(Which

(Which all the gods avert, whom Egypt worſhips)
This infant's life can never ſerve their cauſe,
Nor can his ſingle death prevent their greatneſs.

MELITA.

I know not that : by weakeſt inſtruments
Sometimes are great events produc'd ; this child
Perhaps may live to ſerve his upſtart race
More than an hoſt.

PRINCESS.

How ill does it beſeem
Thy tender years, and gentle womanhood,
To ſteel thy breaſt to Pity's ſacred touch !
So weak, ſo unprotected is our ſex,
So conſtantly expos'd, ſo very helpleſs ;
That did not Heav'n itſelf enjoin compaſſion,
Yet human policy ſhou'd make us kind,
Leſt we ſhou'd need the pity we refuſe.
Yes, I will ſave him——lead me to the place ;
And from the feeble ruſhes we'll remove
The little ark, which cradles this poor babe.

[*The* PRINCESS *and her Maid go out.*

MIRIAM *comes forward.*

How poor were words, to ſpeak my boundleſs joy !
The Princeſs will protect him ; bleſs her, Heav'n !

[*She looks out after the Princeſs, and deſcribes her
action.*

With what impatient ſteps ſhe ſeeks the ſhore !.
Now ſhe approaches where the ark is laid !
With what compaſſion, with what angel-ſweetneſs,

She

She bends to look upon the infant's face!
She takes his little hand in her's —he wakes—
She fmiles upon him—hark! alas, he cries;
Weep on, fweet babe! weep on, till thou haft touch'd
Each chord of pity, waken'd every fenfe
Of melting fympathy, and ftolen her foul!
She takes him in her arms—O lovely Princefs!
How goodnefs heightens beauty! now fhe clafps him
With fondnefs to her heart, fhe gives him now
With tender caution to her damfel's arms:
She points her to the palace, and again
This way the Princefs bends her gracious fteps;
The virgin train retire, and bear the child.

Re-enter the PRINCESS.

PRINCESS.

Did ever innocence and infant-beauty
Plead with fuch dumb but powerful eloquence?
If I, a ftranger, feel thefe foft emotions,
What muft the mother who expos'd him feel!
Go, fetch a woman of the Hebrew race,
That fhe may nurfe the babe; and, by her garb,
Lo fuch a one is here!

MIRIAM.
.Princefs, all hail!
Forgive the bold intrufion of thy fervant,
Who ftands a charm'd fpectator of thy goodnefs.

PRINCESS.
I have redeem'd an infant from the waves,
Whom I intend to nurture as mine own.
                              MIRIAM

MIRIAM.

My tranfports will betray me! [*Afide.*] Gen'rous
Princefs !

PRINCESS.

Know'ft thou a matron of the Hebrew race,
To whom I may confide him ?

MIRIAM.

Well I know
A prudent matron of the houfe of Levi;
Her name is Jochebed, the wife of Amram;
Gentle fhe is, and fam'd throughout her tribe
For foft humanity; full well I know
That fhe will rear him with a mother's love.
[*Afide.*] Oh truly fpoke! a mother's love indeed!
To her defpairing arms I mean to give
This precious truft; the nurfe fhall be the mother!

PRINCESS.

With fpeed conduct this matron to the palace.
Yes, I will raife him up to princely greatnefs,
And he fhall be my fon; his name be *Mofes*,
For I have drawn him from the perilous flood.

[*They go out. She kneels.*

Thou Great Unfeen! thou caufeft gentle deeds.
And fmil'ft on what thou caufeft; thus I blefs thee,
That thou didft deign confult the tender make
Of yielding human hearts, when thou ordain'd'ft
Humanity a virtue! Did'ft incline
That nat'ral bias of the foul to mercy,
Then mad'ft that mercy duty! Gracious Pow'r

Mad'ft

Mad'ſt the keen rapture exquiſite as right :
Beyond the joys of ſenſe ; as pleaſure ſweet ;
As reaſon conſtant, and as inſtinct ſtrong !

MOSES IN THE BULRUSHES:

PART III.

Enter JOCHEBED.

I'VE almoſt reach'd the place—with cautious ſteps
1 muſt approach to where the ark is laid,
Leſt from the royal gardens any ſpy me.
—Poor babe ! ere this, the preſſing calls of hunger
Have broke thy ſhort repoſe ; the chilling waves,
Perhaps, have drench'd thy little ſhiv'ring limbs.
What—what muſt he have ſuffer'd !—No one ſees me :
But ſoft, does no one liſten ?—Ah ! how hard,
How very hard for fondneſs to be prudent !
Now is the moment, to embrace and feed him.

[*She looks out.*
Where's

Where's Miriam? she has left her little charge,
Perhaps through fear, perhaps she was detected.
How wild is thought! how terrible conjecture!
A mother's fondness frames a thousand fears,
And shapes unreal evils into being.

> [*She looks towards the river.*

Ah me! where is he? foul-distracting sight!
He is not there—he's lost, he's gone, he's drown'd!
Tofs'd by each beating furge my infant floats;
Cold, cold and wat'ry is thy grave, my child!
O no—I fee the ark—Tranfporting fight;

> [*She goes towards it.*

What do I fee? Alas, the ark is empty!
The cafket's left, the precious gem is gone!
You fpar'd him, pitying fpirits of the deep!
But vain your mercy; fome infatiate beaft,
Cruel as Pharaoh, took the life you fpar'd—
And I fhall never, never fee him more!

Enter MIRIAM.

JOCHEBED.
Come, and lament with me thy brother's lofs!

MIRIAM.
Come, and adore with me the GOD of Jacob!

JOCHEBED.
Miriam—the child is dead!

MIRIAM.
> He lives, he lives!

E   JOCHEBED.

JOCHEBED.

Impoffible: Oh! do not mock my grief!
See'ft thou that empty veffel?

MIRIAM.

From that veffel
Th' Egyptian Princefs took him.

JOCHEBED.

Pharaoh's daugher?
Then ftill he will be flain.

MIRIAM.

His life is fafe;
For know, fhe means to rear him as her own.

JOCHEBED.

[*Falls on her knees in rapture.*
To GOD the LORD, the glory be afcrib'd!
Oh magnified for ever be thy might,
Who mercy in a Heathen's heart can'ft plant,
And from the depth of evil bring forth good!

[*She rifes.*

MIRIAM.

O bleft event, beyond our warmeft hopes.

JOCHEBED.

What! fhall my fon be nurtur'd in a court,
In princely grandeur bred? taught every art,
And every wond'rous fcience Egypt knows?
Yet ah! I tremble, Miriam; fhou'd he learn,
With Egypt's polifh'd arts, her baneful faith!

O worfe

O worfe exchange for death! Yes, fhou'd he learn
In yon' proud palace to difown *his* hand
Who thus has fav'd him : fhou'd he e'er embrace
(As fure he will, if bred in Pharaoh's court)
The grofs idolatries which Egypt owns,
Her graven images, her brutifh gods :
Then fhall I wifh he had not been preferv'd,
To fhame his fathers, and deny his faith.

M I R I A M.

Then, to difpel thy fears, and crown thy joy,
Hear farther wonders—Know, the gen'rous Princefs
To thine own care thy darling child commits.

J O C H E B E D.

Speak, while my joy will give me time to liften!

M I R I A M.

By her commiffion'd, thou behold'ft me here,
To feek a matron of the Hebrew race,
To nurfe him; thou, my mother, art that matron.——
I faid, I knew thee well; that thou wou'd'ft rear him
Ev'n with a mother's fondnefs; fhe, who bare him,
(I told the Princefs) could not love him more.

J O C H E B E D.

Fountain of Mercy! whofe pervading eye
Beholds the heart, and fees what paffes there,
Accept my thoughts for thanks! I have no words—
How poor were human language to exprefs
My gratitude, my wonder, and my joy!

MIRIAM.

MIRIAM.

Yes, thou fhalt pour into his infant mind
The pureft precepts of the pureft faith.

JOCHEBED.

O! I will fill his tender foul with virtue,
And warm his bofom with devotion's flame!
Aid me, celeftial Spirit! with thy grace,
And be my labours with thy influence crown'd:
Without it they were vain. Then, then, my Miriam,
When he is furnifh'd, 'gainft the evil day,
With God's whole armour*, girt with facred truth,
And as a breaft-plate, wearing righteoufnefs,
Arm'd with the fpirit of God, the fhield of Faith,
And with the helmet of falvation crown'd,
Inur'd to watching, and difpos'd to pray'r;
Then may I fend him to a dangerous court,
And fafely truft him in a perilous world,
Too full of tempting fnares and fond delufions!

MIRIAM.

May bounteous Heav'n, thy pious cares reward!

JOCHEBED.

O Amram! O my hufband! when thou com'ft,
Wearied at night, to reft thee from the toils
Impos'd by haughty Pharaoh; what a tale
Have I to tell thee! yes——thy darling fon
Was loft, and is reftor'd; was dead, and lives!

MIRIAM.

---

* 2 Thef. chap. v. Alfo, Ephef. chap. vi.

MIRIAM.

How joyful fhall we fpend the live-long night
In praifes to JEHOVAH; who thus mocks
All human forefight, and converts the means
Of feeming ruin into great deliverance!

JOCHEBED.

Had not my child been doom'd to fuch ftrange perils,
As a fond mother trembles to recall;
He had not been preferv'd.

MIRIAM.

And mark ftill farther:
Had he been fav'd by any other hand,
He had been ftill expos'd to equal ruin.

JOCHEBED.

Then let us join to blefs the hand of Heaven,
That this poor outcaft of the houfe of Ifrael,
Condemn'd to die by Pharaoh, kept in fecret
By my advent'rous fondnefs; then expos'd
Ev'n by that very fondnefs which conceal'd him,
Is now, to fill the wondrous round of mercy,
Preferv'd from perifhing by Pharaoh's daughter,
Sav'd by the very hand which fought to crufh him!

Wife and unfearchable are all thy ways,
Thou GOD of MERCIES!—Lead me to my child!

THE END.

PERSONS of the DRAMA.

SAUL, King of Israel.
ABNER, his General.
JESSE.
ELIAB,
ABINADAB, } Sons of Jesse.
DAVID,
GOLIATH, the Philistine Giant.
Philistines, Israelites, &c. &c.

Chorus of Hebrew Women.

The SCENE lies in the Camp, in the Valley of
Elah and the adjacent Plain.

☞ The Subject of the Drama is taken from the Seven-
teenth Chapter of the First Book of Samuel.

DAVID AND GOLIATH.

A

SACRED DRAMA.

PART I.

O bienheureux mille fois,
L'Enfant que le Seigneur aime,
Que de bonne heure entend fa voix,
Et que ce Dieu daigne inftruire lui-même!
Loin du monde élevé ; de tous les dons des Cieux,
Il eft orné dès fa naiffance ;
Et du méchant l'abord contagieux
N'altere point fon innocence.——ATHALIE.

SCENE, à Shepherd's Tent on a Plain.

DAVID, *under a fpreading tree, plays on his harp, and fings.*

I.

GREAT Lord of all things ! Pow'r divine !
Breathe on this erring heart of mine
Thy grace ferene and pure ;
Defend my frail, my erring youth,
And teach me this important truth,
The humble are fecure.

II.

II.

Teach me to blefs my lowly lot
Confin'd to this paternal cot,
    Remote from regal ftate ;
Content to court the cooling glade,
Inhale the breeze, enjoy the fhade,
    And love my humble fate.

III.

No anxious vigils here I keep,
No dreams of gold diftract my fleep,
    Nor lead my heart aftray ;
Nor blafting Envy's tainted gale
Pollutes the pleafures of the vale,
    To vex my harmlefs day.

IV.

Yon' tow'r, which rears its head fo high,
And bids defiance to the fky,
    Invites the hoftile winds :
Yon' branching oak extending wide,
Provokes deftruction by its pride,
    And courts the fall it finds.

V.

Then let me fhun th' ambitious deed,
And all the dangerous paths which lead
    To honours falfely won :
Lord! in thy fure protection bleft,
Submiffive will I ever reft,
    And may thy will be done!
        [*He lays down his harp, and rifes.*

DAVID.

DAVID.

This Shepherd's life were dull and taftelefs all,
Without the charm of foothing fong or harp:
With it, not undelightful is the haunt
Of wood, or lonely grove, or ruffet plain,
Made vocal by the Mufe. With this lov'd harp,
This daily folace of my cares, I footh'd
The melancholy monarch, when he lay,
Smit by the chill and fpirit-quenching hand
Of blank defpair. GOD of my fathers! hear me:
Here I devote my harp, my verfe, myfelf,
To thy bleft fervice! gladly to proclaim
Glory to GOD on high, on earth good-will
To man; to pour my grateful foul before thee;
To fing thy pow'r, thy wifdom, and thy love,
And every gracious attribute: to paint
The charms of heav'n-born virtue! So fhall I,
(Tho with long interval of worth) afpire
To imitate the work of faints above,
Of Cherub and of Seraphim. My heart,
My talents, all I am, and all I have,
Is thine, O Father! Gracious LORD, accept
The humble dedication! Offer'd gifts
Of flaughter'd bulls, and goats facrificial,
Thou haft refus'd: but lo! I come, O LORD,
To do thy will! the living facrifice
Of an obedient heart I lay before thee!
This humble off'ring more fhall pleafe thee, LORD!
Than horned bullocks, ceremonial rites,
New moons, appointed paffovers, and fafts!
Yet thofe I too will keep; but not inftead
Of holinefs fubftantial, inward worth;

F   As

As commutation cheap for pious deeds,
And purity of life. But as the types
Of better things ; as fair external figns
Of inward holinefs and fecret truth.

But fee, my father, good old Jeffe comes !
To cheer the fetting evening of whofe life,
Content, a fimple fhepherd here I dwell,
Tho' Ifrael is in arms , and royal Saul
Encamp'd in yonder field, defies Philiftia.

JESSE, DAVID.

JESSE.

Bleft be the gracious Pow'r, who gave my age
To boaft a fon like thee!   Thou art the ftaff
Which props my bending years, and makes me bear
The heavy burthen of declining age
With fond complacence.   How unlike thy fate,
O venerable Eli ! But two fons,
But only two, to gild the dim remains
Of life's departing day, and blefs thy age,
And both were curfes to thee ! Witnefs, Heav'n !
In all the tedious catalogue of pains
Humanity turns o'er, if there be one
So terrible to human tendernefs,
As an unnatural child !

DAVID.

O, my lov'd father !
Long may'ft thou live, in years and honours rich ;
To tafte, and to communicate the joys,
The thoufand fond, endearing charities

Of tendernefs domeftic; Nature's beft
And lovelieft gift, with which fhe well atones
The niggard boon of fortune.

JESSE.
                         O, my fon!
Of all the graces which adorn thy youth,
I, with a father's fondnefs, muft commend
Thy tried humility. For tho' the Seer
Pour'd on thy chofen head the facred oil,
In fign of future greatnefs, in fure pledge
Of higheft dignity; yet here thou dwell'ft,
Content with toil, and carelefs of repofe;
And (harder ftill for an ingenuous mind)
Content to be obfcure : content to watch,
With careful eye, thine humble father's flock!'
O, earthly emblem of celeftial things!
'So Ifrael's fhepherd watches o'er his fold:
The weak ones in his foft'ring bofom bears;
And gently leads, in his fuftaining hand,
The feeble ones with young.

DAVID.
                    Know'ft thou, my father,
Ought from the field? for tho' fo near the camp,
Tho' war's proud enfigns ftream on yonder plain,
And all Philiftia's fwarming hofts encamp,
Oppos'd to royal Saul, beneath whofe banners
My brothers lift the fpear; I have not left
My fleecy charge, by thee committed to me,
To learn the prefent fortune of the war.

JESSE.

JESSE.

And wifely haft thou done.   Thrice happy realm,
Who fhall fubmit one day to his command
Who can fo well obey! Obedience leads
To certain honours.   Not the tow'ring wing
Of eagle-plum'd ambition mounts fo furely
To Fortune's higheft fummit, as odedience.

[*A diftant found of trumpets.*

But why that fudden ardour, O my fon?
That trumpet's found (tho' fo remote its voice,
We hardly catch the echo as it dies)
Has rous'd the mantling crimfon in thy cheek:
Kindled the martial fpirit in thine eye,
And my young fhepherd feels an hero's fire!

DAVID.

Thou haft not told the pofture of the war,
And much my beating bofom pants to hear.

JESSE.

Uncertain is the fortune of the field.
I tremble for thy brothers, thus expos'd
To conftant peril, nor for them alone,
Does the quick feeling agonize my heart.
I too lament, that defolating war
Hangs his fell banner o'er my native land,
Belov'd Jerufalem! O war, what art thou?
After the brighteft conqueft, what remains
Of all thy glories? For the vanquifh'd, chains!
For the proud victor, what? Alas! to reign
O'er defolated nations! a drear wafte,
By one man's crime, by one man's luft of pow'r,
Unpeopled! Naked plains and ravag'd fields

Succeed

Succeed to smiling harvests, and the fruits
Of peaceful olive, luscious fig and vine!
Here, rifled temples are the cavern'd dens
Of savage beasts, or haunt of birds obscene.
There, populous cities blacken in the sun,
And, in the gen'ral wreck, proud palaces
Lie undistinguish'd, save by the dun smoke
Of recent conflagration.   When the song
Of dear-bought joy, with many a triumph swell'd,
Salutes the victor's ear, and sooths his pride;
How is the grateful harmony profan'd
With the sad dissonance of virgins' cries,
Who mourn their brothers slain! Of matrons hoar,
Who clasp their wither'd hands, and fondly ask,
With iteration shrill, their slaughter'd sons!
How is the laurel's verdure stain'd with blood,
And foil'd with widows' tears!

DAVID.
　　　　　　　Thrice mournful truth!
Yet when our country's rights, her sacred laws,
Her holy faith are scorn'd and trampled on,
Then, then religion calls; then God himself
Commands us to defend his injur'd name.
'Twere then inglorious weakness, mean self-love,
To lie inactive, when the stirring voice
Of the shrill trumpet wakes to desp'rate deeds;
Nor with heroic valour boldly dare
Th' idolatrous heathen bands, ev'n to the death.

JESSE.
God and thy country claim the life they gave,
No other cause can sanctify resentment.

DAVID.

DAVID.

Sure virtuous friendſhip is a noble cauſe!
O were the princely Jonathan in danger,
How wou'd I die, well-pleas'd, in his'defence!
When ('twas long ſince, then but a ſtripling boy)
I made ſhort ſojourn in his father's palace,
(At firſt to ſooth his troubled mind with ſong,
His armour-bearer next;) I well remember
The gracious bounties of the gallant prince.
How wou'd he ſit, attentive to my ſtrain;
While to my harp I ſung the harmleſs joys,
Which crown a ſhepherd's life! How wou'd he cry,
"Bleſs'd youth, far happier in thy native worth,
Far richer in the talent Heav'n has lent thee,
Than if a crown hung o'er thy anxious brow.,
The jealous monarch mark'd our growing friendſhip;
And as my favour grew with thoſe about him,
His royal bounty leſſen'd, till at length,
For Bethl'hem's ſafer ſhades I left the court.
Nor wou'd theſe alter'd features now be known,
Grown into manly ſtrength; nor this chang'd form,.
Enlarg'd with age, and clad in ruſſet weed.

JESSE.

I have employment for thee, my lov'd ſon,
Will pleaſe thy active ſpirit. Go, my boy!
Haſte to the field of war, to yonder camp,
Where, in the vale of Elah, mighty Saul'
Commands the hoſts of Iſrael.   Greet thy brothers;
Obſerve their deeds; note their demeanor well;
And mark if wiſdom on their actions waits.
Bear to them too (for well the waſte of war
Will make it needful) ſuch plain healthful viands,

As

As furnifh out our frugal fhepberd's meal.
And to the valiant captain of their hoft,
Prefent fuch rural gifts as fuit our fortune.
Heap'd on the board within my tent thou'lt find them.

DAVID.

With joy I'll bear thy prefents to my brothers;
And to the valiant captain of their hoft,
The rural gifts thy gratitude affigns him.
What tranfport to behold the tented field,
The pointed fpear, the blaze of fhields and arms,
And all the proud accoutrements of war!
But, oh! far dearer tranfport would it yield me,
Cou'd this right arm alone avenge the caufe
Of injur'd Ifrael, and preferve the lives
Of guiltlefs thoufands, doom'd perhaps to bleed!

JESSE.

Let not thy youth be dazzled, O my fon!
With deeds of bold emprize, as valour only
Were virtue; and the gentle arts of peace,
Of truth and juftice, were not worth thy care.
When thou fhalt view the fplendors of the war,
The gay caparifon, the burnifh'd fhield,
The plume-crown'd helmet, and the glitt'ring fpear,
Scorn not the humble virtues of the fhade;
Nor think that Heav'n views only with applaufe
The active merit, and the bufy toil
Of heroes, ftatefmen, and the buftling fons
Of public care. Thefe have their juft reward
In wealth, in honours, and the well-earn'd fame
Their high atchievements bring. 'Tis in this view,
That virtue is her proper recompence.

Wealth,

Wealth, as its natural confequence, will flow
From induftry; toil with fuccefs is crown'd :
From fplendid actions high renown will fpring. *
Such is the ufual courfe of human things.
For Wifdom Infinite permits, that thus
Effects to caufes be proportionate,
And nat'ral ends by nat'ral means atchiev'd.
But in the future eftimate, which Heav'n
Will make of things terreftrial, know, my fon,
That no inferior bleffing is referv'd
For the mild *paffive* virtues; meek Content,
Heroic Self-denial, nobler far
Than all th' atchievements noify Fame reports,
When her fhrill trump proclaims the proud fuccefs
Which defolates the nations. But, on earth,
Thefe are not always fortunate; becaufe
Eternal Juftice keeps them for the blifs
Of final recompence, for the dread day
Of gen'ral retribution. O my fon !
The oftentatious virtues, which ftill prefs
For notice, and for praife; the brilliant deeds,
Which live but in the eye of obfervation,
Thefe have their meed at once. But there's a joy,
To the fond votaries of Fame unknown ;
To hear the ftill fmall voice of confcience fpeak
Its whifp'ring plaudit to the filent foul.
Heav'n notes the figh afflicted Goodnefs heaves ;
Hears the low plaint by human ear unheard,
And from the cheek of patient Sorrow wipes
The tear, by mortal eye unfeen or fcorn'd.

DAVID.

DAVID.

As Hermon's dews their grateful freſhneſs ſhed,
And cheer the herbage, and the flow'rs renew;
So do thy words a quick'ning balm infuſe,
And grateful ſink in my delighted ſoul.

JESSE.

Go then, my child! and may the Gracious GOD,
Who bleſs'd our fathers, bleſs my much-lov'd ſon!

DAVID.

Farewell, my father! and of this be ſure,
That not a precept from thy honour'd lips
Shall fall, by me unnoticed; not one grace,
One venerable virtue, which adorns
Thy daily life, but I, with watchful care,
And due-obſervance, will in mine tranſplant it.

[*Exit* DAVID.

JESSE.

He's gone! and ſtill my aching eyes purſue,
And ſtrain their orbs ſtill longer to behold him.
Oh! who can tell, when I may next embrace him?
Who can declare the counſels of the Lord?
Or when the moment pre-ordain'd by Heav'n
To fill his great deſigns may come? This ſon,
This bleſſing of my age, is ſet apart
For high exploits; the choſen inſtrument
Of all-diſpoſing Heav'n for mighty deeds.
Still I recal the day, and to my mind
The ſcene is ever preſent; when the Seer,
Illuſtrious Samuel, to the humble ſhades
Of Bethlehem came, pretending ſacrifice,
To ſcreen his errand from the jealous king.

G   He

He fanctify'd us firft, me, and my fons ;
For fanctity increas'd fhould ftill precede
Increafe of dignity.   When he declar'd
He came, commiffion'd from on High, to find,
Among the fons of Jeffe, Ifrael's king ;
Aftonifhment entranc'd my wond'ring foul.
Yet was it not a wild tumultuous blifs ;
Such rafh delight as promis'd honours yield
To light, vain minds ; no, 'twas a doubtful joy
Chaftis'd by tim'rous virtue, left a gift
So fplendid, and fo dang'rous, might deftroy
Him it was meant to raife.   My eldeft born,
Young Eliab, tall of ftature, I prefented ;
But God, who judges not by outward form,
But tries the heart, forbad the holy prophet
To chufe my eldeft born.   For Saul, he faid,
Gave proof, that fair proportion, and the grace
Of limb or feature, ill repaid the want
Of virtue.   All my other fons alike
By Samuel were rejected : till, at laft,
On my young boy, on David's chofen head,
The prophet pour'd the confecrated oil.
Yet ne'er did pride elate him, ne'er did fcorn
For his rejected elders fwell his heart.
Not in fuch gentle charity to him
His haughtier brothers live : but all he pardons.
To meditation, and to humble toil,
To pray'r, and praife devoted, here he dwells.
O may the Graces which adorn retreat,
One day delight a court ! record his name
With faints and prophets, dignify his race,
Inftruct mankind, and fanctify a world !

DAVID

DAVID AND GOLIATH.

PART II.

SCENE, The Camp.

ELIAB, ABINADAB, ABNER, ISRAELITES.

ELIAB.

STILL is the event of this long war uncertain:
Still do the adverse hosts, on either side,
Protract, with ling'ring caution, an encounter,
Which must to one be fatal.

ABINADAB.
This descent,
Thus to the very confines of our land,
Proclaims the sanguine hope that fires the foe.
In Ephes-dammim boldly they encamp:
Th' uncircumcis'd Philistines pitch their tents
On Judah's hallow'd earth.

G 2

ELIAB.

ELIAB.

Full forty days.
Has the infulting giant, proud Goliath,
The champion of Philiftia, fiercely challeng'd.
Some Ifraelitifh foe.   But who fo vain
To dare fuch force unequal? who fo bent
On fure deftruction, to accept his terms;
And rufh on death, beneath the giant force,,
Of, his enormous bulk?

ABINADAB.

'Tis near the time,.
When, in th' adjacent valley which divides
Th' oppofing armies, he is wont to make
His daily challenge.

ELIAB.

Much I marvel, brother!
No greetings from our father reach our ears.
With eafe and plenty blefs'd, he little recks
The daily hardfhips which his fons endure.
But fee! behold his darling fon approaches!

ABINADAB.

How, David here? whence this unlook'd-for gueft?

ELIAB.

A fpy upon our actions; fent no doubt,.
To fcan our deeds, with beardlefs gravity
Affecting wifdom; to obferve each word,.
To magnify the venial faults of youth,
And conftrue harmlefs mirth to foul offence.

Enter DAVID.

DAVID.

All hail, my deareſt brothers!

ELIAB.

Means thy greeting
True love, or arrogant ſcorn?

DAVID.

Oh, moſt true love!
Sweet as the precious ointment, which bedew'd
The ſacred head of Aaron, and deſcended
Upon his hallow'd veſt; ſo ſweet, my brothers,
Is fond fraternal amity; ſuch love
As my touch'd boſom feels at your approach.

ELIAB.

Still that fine glozing ſpeech, thoſe holy ſaws,
And all that trick of ſtudied ſanctity,
Of ſmooth-turn'd periods, and trim eloquence,
Which charms thy doating father. But confeſs,
What doſt thou here? Is it to ſoothe thy pride,
And gratify thy vain deſire to roam,
In queſt of pleaſures unallow'd? or com'ſt thou,
A willing ſpy, to note thy brother's deeds?
Where haſt thou left thoſe few poor ſtraggling ſheep?
More ſuited to thy ignorance and years
The care of thoſe, than here to wander idly.
Why cam'ſt thou hither?

DAVID.

DAVID.

Is there not a cauſe?
Why that diſpleaſure kindling in thine eye,
My angry brother? why thoſe taunts unkind?
Not idly bent on ſport; not to delight
Mine eye with all this gay parade of war;
To gratify a roving appetite,
Or fondly to indulge a curious ear
With any tale of rumour, am I come :
But to approve myſelf a loving brother.
I bring the bleſſing of your aged ſire.
With gifts of ſuch plain cates, and rural viands,
As ſuit his frugal fortune. Tell me now,
Where the bold captain of your hoſt encamps?

ELIAB.

Wherefore enquire? what boots it thee to know?
Behold him there: great Abner, fam'd in arms.

DAIVD.

I bring thee, mighty Abner, from my father,
(A ſimple ſhepherd ſwain in yonder vale)
Such humble gifts as ſhepherd ſwains beſtow.

ABNER.

Thanks, gentle youth! with pleaſure I receive
The grateful off'ring. Why does thy quick eye
Thus wander with unſatisfied delight?

DAVID.

New as I am to all the trade of war,
Each ſound has novelty; each thing I ſee
Attracts attention; every noiſe I hear

Awakes

Awakes confus'd emotions; indiftinct,
Yet full of charming tumult, fweet diftraction.
'Tis all delightful hurry! Oh! the joy
Of young ideas painted on the mind,
In the warm glowing colours fancy fpreads
On objects not yet known, when all is new,
And all is lovely! Ah! what warlike found
Salutes my ravifh'd ear?

[Sound of trumpet.

ABNER.
      'Tis the Philiftine,
Proclaming, by his herald, through the ranks,
His near approach. Each morning he repeats
His challenge to our bands.

DAVID.
      Ha! what Philiftine?
Who is he?

ELIAB.
      Wherefore afk? for thy raw youth,
And ruftic ignorance, 'twere fitter learn
Some rural art; fome fecret to prevent
Contagion in thy flocks; fome better means
To fave their fleece immaculate. Thefe mean arts,
Of foft inglorious peace, far better fuit
Thy low obfcurity, than thus to feek
High things, pertaining to exploits of arms.

DAVID.
Urg'd as I am, I will not anfwer thee.
Who conquers his own fpirit, O my brother!

He

He is the only conqueror.—Again
That fhout myfterious! Pray you, tell me who
This proud Philiftine is, who fends defiance
To Ifrael's hardy chieftains?

ABNER.
Stranger youth!
So lovely and fo mild is thy demeanour,
So gentle, and fo patient; fuch the air
Of candor and of courage, which adorns
Thy blooming features, thou haft won my love;
And I will tell thee.

DAVID.
Mighty Abner! thanks!

ABNER.
Thrice, and no more, he founds, his daily rule.
This man of war, this champion of Philiftia,
Is of the fons of Anak's giant-race.
Goliath is his name. His fearful ftature,
Unparallel'd in Ifrael, meafures more
Than twice three cubits. On his tow'ring head
A helm of burnifh'd brafs the giant wears,
So pond'rous, it would crufh the ftouteft man
In all our hofts. A coat of mailed armour
Guards his capacious trunk; compar'd with which
The ampleft oak, that fpreads his rugged arms
In Bafhan's groves, were fmall. About his neck
A fhining corflet hangs. On his vaft thigh
The plaited cuirafs firmly jointed ftands.
But who fhall tell the wonders of his fpear,

And hope to gain belief? of maffive iron
Its temper'd frame; not lefs than the broad beam
To which the bufy weaver hangs his loom;
Not to be wielded by a mortal hand,
Save by his own. An armour-bearer walks
Before this mighty champion, in his hand
Bearing the giant's fhield. Thrice, every morn,
His herald founds the trumpet of defiance;
Off'ring at once to end the long-drawn war,
In fingle combat, 'gainft that hardy foe
Who dares encounter him.

DAVID.

Say, mighty Abner!
What are the haughty terms of his defiance?

ABNER.

Proudly he ftalks around th' extremeft bounds
Of Elah's valley. His herald founds the note
Of offer'd battle. Then the furious giant,
With fuch a voice as from the troubled fky,
In vollied thunder, breaks, thus fends his challenge:
" Why do you fet your battle in array,
Ye men of Ifrael? Wherefore wafte the lives
Of needlefs thoufands? Why protract a war,
Which may at once be ended? Are not you
Servants to Saul your king? and am not I,
With triumph let me fpeak it, a Philiftine?
Chufe out a man from all your armed hofts,
Of courage moft approv'd; and I will meet him,
His fingle arm to mine. Th' event of this
Shall fix the fate of Ifrael and Philiftia.

H

If victory favour him, then will we live
Your tributary flaves; but if my arm
Be crown'd with conqueft, you fhall then live ours.
Give me a man, if your effeminate bands
A man can boaft. Your armies I defy."

DAVID.
What fhall be done to him, who fhall fubdue
This vile idolater?

ABNER.
He fhall receive
Such ample bounties, fuch profufe rewards,
As might inflame chill age, or cowardice,
Were not the odds fo defperate.

DAVID.
Say, what are they?

ABNER.
The royal Saul has promis'd that bold hero,
Who fhall encounter and fubdue Goliath,
All dignity and favour; that his houfe
Shall be fet free from tribute, and ennobled
With the firft honours Ifrael has to give.
And for the gallant conqueror himfelf,
No lefs a recompence than the fair Princefs,
Our monarch's peerlefs daughter.

DAVID.
Beauteous Michal!
It is indeed a boon which kings might ftrive for.
And has none anfwer'd yet this bold defiance?

What

What, all this goodly hoft of Ifraelites,
God's own peculiar people! all afraid
T' affert God's injur'd honour, and their own ?
The king himfelf, who in his early youth
Wrought deeds of fame! the princely Jonathan!
Not fo the gallant youth Philiftia fear'd
At Bozez and at Seneh *; when the earth
Shook from her deep foundations, to behold
The wond'rous carnage of his fingle hand
On the uncircumcis'd. When he exclaim'd,
With glorious confidence—" Shall numbers awe me ?
" God will protect his own : with him to fave,
" It boots not, friends, by many or by few."
This was an heroe! Why does he delay
To meet this boafter ? For thy courtefy,
Thrice noble Abner, I am bound to thank thee!
Wou'd'ft thou complete thy gen'rous offices ?
I dare not afk it.

ABNER.
Speak thy wifhes freely:
My foul inclines to ferve thee.

DAVID.
Then, O Abner,
Conduct me to the king! There is a caufe
Will juftify this boldnefs.

ELIAB.
Braggard, hold!

H 2   ABNER.

---

* 1 *Samuel* xiv.

ABNER.

I take thee at thy word; and will, with speed,
Conduct thee to my royal master's presence.
In yonder tent, the anxious monarch waits
Th' event of this day's challenge.

DAVID.

     Noble Abner!
Accept my thanks. Now to thy private ear,
If so thy grace permit, I will unfold
My secret soul ; and ease my lab'ring breast,
Which pants with high designs, and beats for glory.

DAVID AND GOLIATH.

PART III.

SCENE, Saul's Tent.

SAUL.

WHY was I made a king ? what I have gain'd
In envy'd greatness and uneasy pow'r,
I've lost in peace of mind, in virtue lost !
Why did deceitful transports fire my soul,
When Samuel plac'd upon my youthful brow
The crown of Israel ? I had known content,
Nay happiness, if happiness unmix'd

        To;

To mortal man were known; had I ftill liv'd
Among the humble tents of Benjamin.
A fhepherd's occupation was my joy,
And ev'ry guiltlefs day was crown'd with peace.
But now, a fullen cloud for ever hangs
O'er the faint funfhine of my brighteft hours,
Dark'ning the golden promife of the morn.
I ne'er fhall tafte the dear domeftic joys
My meaneft fubjects know. True, I have fons,
Whofe virtues would have charm'd a private man,
And drawn down bleffings on their humble fire.
I love their virtues too; but 'tis a love,
Which jealoufy has poifon'd. Jonathan
Is all a father's fondnefs cou'd conceive
Of amiable and good——Of that no more!
He is too popular; the people doat
Upon th' ingenuous graces of his youth.
Curs'd popularity! which makes a father
Deteft the merit of a fon he loves.
How did their fond idolatry perforce,
Refcue his fentenc'd life, when doom'd by lot
To perifh at Beth-aven*, for the breach
Of ftrict injunction, that of all my bands,
Not one that day fhou'd tafte of food, and live.
My fubjects clamour at this tedious war,
Yet of my num'rous armed chiefs, not one
Has courage to engage-this man of Gath.
O for a champion bold enough to face
This giant-boafter, whofe repeated threats
Strike thro' my inmoft foul! There was a time——

Of

* 1 *Samuel*, xiv.

Of that no more !——I am not what I was.
Shou'd valiant Jonathan accept the challenge,
'Twould but increafe his favour with the people,
And make the crown fit loofely on my brow.
Ill cou'd my wounded fpirit brook the voice
Of harfh comparifon 'twixt fire and fon.

SAUL, ABNER.

ABNER.

What meditation holds thee thus engag'd,
O king ! and keeps thine active fpirit bound ;
When bufy war far other cares demands
Than ruminating thought, and pale defpair ?

SAUL.

Abner, draw near.   My weary foul finks down
Beneath the heavy preffure of misfortune.   .
O for that fpirit, which inflam'd my breaft
With fudden fervor ; when among the feers,
And holy fages, my prophetic voice
Was heard attentive, and th' aftonifh'd throng,
Wond'ring, exclaim'd, " Is Saul among the prophets ?"
Where's that bold arm which quell'd th' Amalekite,
And nobly fpar'd fierce Agag and his flocks ?
'Tis paft ; the light of Ifrael now is quench'd :
Shorn of his beams, my fun of glory fets !
Rife Mcab, Edom, angry Ammon, rife !
Come Gaza, Afhdod come ! let Ekron boaft,
And Afkelon rejoice, for Saul——is nothing.

ABNER.

I bring thee news, O king !

SAUL.

My valiant uncle!
What can avail thy news? A soul oppress'd,
Refuses still to hear the charmer's voice,
Howe'er enticingly he charm. What news
Can sooth my sickly soul, while Gath's fell giant
Repeats each morning to my frighten'd hosts
His daring challenge—none accepting it?

ABNER.

It is accepted.

SAUL.

Ha! by whom? how? when?
What prince, what gen'ral, what illustrious hero,
What vet'ran chief, what warrior of renown,
Will dare to meet the haughty foe's defiance?
Speak, my brave gen'ral! noble Abner, speak!

ABNER.

No prince, no warrior, no illustrious chief,
No vet'ran hero dares accept the challenge;
But what will move thy wonder, mighty king!
One train'd to peaceful deeds, and new to arms,
A simple shepherd swain.

SAUL.

O mockery!
No more of this light tale, it suits but ill
Thy bearded gravity: or rather tell it
To credulous age, or weak believing women;
They love whate'er is marvellous, and doat

On

On deeds prodigious, and incredible,
Which fober fenfe rejects. I laugh to think
Of thy extravagance. A fhepherd's boy
Encounter him, whom nations dread to meet!

ABNER.

Is valour, then, peculiar to high birth?
If Heav'n had fo decreed, know, fcornful king,
That Saul the Benjamite had never reign'd.
No:—Glory darts her foul-pervading ray,
On thrones and cottages, regardlefs ftill
Of all the falfe, chimerical diftinctions
Vain human cuftoms make.

SAUL.
Where is this youth?

ABNER.

Without thy tent he waits. Such humble fweetnefs,
Fir'd with the fecret confcience of defert;
Such manly bearing, tempered with fuch foftnefs,
And fo adorn'd with every outward charm
Of graceful form and feature, faw I never.

SAUL.

Bring me the youth.

ABNER.
He waits thy royal pleafure.
[*Exit* ABNER.

SAUL.

What muft I think? Abner himfelf is brave,
And fkill'd in human kind: nor does he judge

So

So lightly, to be caught by fpecious words,
And fraud's fmooth artifice, without the mark
Of worth intrinfic. But behold he comes!
The youth too with him! Juftly did he praife
The candor, which adorns his open brow.

Re-enter ABNER *and* DAVID.

DAVID.

Hail, mighty king!

ABNER.

Behold thy proffer'd champion.

SAUL.

Art thou the youth, whofe high heroic zeal
Afpires to meet the giant fon of Anak?

DAVID.

If fo the king permit.

SAUL.

Impoffible!
Why, what experience has thy youth of arms?
Where didft thou learn the dreadful trade of war?
Beneath what hoary vet'ran haft thou ferv'd?
What feats atchiev'd, what deeds of bold emprize?
What well-rang'd phalanx, and what charging hofts,
What hard campaigns, what fieges haft thou feen?
Haft thou e'er fcal'd the city's rampir'd wall,
Or hurl'd the miffile dart, or learn'd to poife
The warrior's deathful fpear? The ufe of targe,
Of helm, and buckler, is to thee unknown.

I   DAVID.

DAVID.

Arms I have feldom feen. I little know
Of war's proud difcipline. The trumpet's clang,
The fhock of charging hofts, the rampir'd wall,
Th' embattled phalanx, and the warrior fpear,
The ufe of targe and helm to me is new.
My zeal for GOD, my patriot love of Ifrael,
And reverence for my king, thefe are my claims.

SAUL.

But, gentle youth, thou haft no fame in arms,
Renown, with her fhrill clarion, never bore
Thy honour'd name to many a land remote.
From the fair regions, where Euphrates laves
Affyria's borders, to the diftant Nile.

DAVID.

True, mighty king! I am indeed alike
Unblefs'd by Fortune, and to Fame unknown;
A lowly fhepherd-fwain of Judah's tribe.
But greatnefs ever fprings from low beginnings.
That very Nile thou mention'ft, whofe broad ftream
Bears fruitfulnefs and health thro' many a clime,
From an unknown, penurious, fcanty fource,
Took its firft rife. The foreft oak, which fhades
Thy fultry troops in many a toilfome march,
Once an unheeded acorn lay. O king!
Who ne'er begins, can never ought atchieve
Of glorious, Thou thyfelf waft once unknown,
'Till fair occafion brought thy worth to light.
Sublimer views infpire my youthful heart,
Than human praife : I feek to vindicate
Th' infulted honour of the GOD thou ferv'ft.

ABNER.

A SACRED DRAMA.

ABNER.

'Tis nobly faid.

SAUL.

I love thy fpirit, youth!
But dare not truft thy inexperienc'd arm
Againft a giant's might. The fight of blood,
Tho' brave thou feel'ft when peril is not nigh,
Will pale thy ardent cheek.

DAVID.

Not fo, O king!
This youthful arm has been imbru'd in blood,
Tho' yet no blood of man has ever ftain'd it.
Thy fervant's occupation is a fhepherd :
With jealous care I watch'd my father's flock :
A brindled lion, and a furious bear,
Forth from the thicket rufh'd upon the fold,
Seiz'd a young lamb, and tore their bleating fpoil ;
Urg'd by compaffion for my helplefs charge,
I felt a new-born vigour nerve my arm,
And, eager, on the foaming monfters rufh'd.
The famifh'd lion by his grifly beard,
Enrag'd, I caught, and fmote him to the ground ;
The panting monfter ftruggling in my gripe,
Shook terribly his briftling mane, and lafh'd
His own gaunt, goary fides; fiercely he ground
His gnafhing teeth, and roll'd his ftarting eyes,
Bloodfhot with agony : then with a groan,
That wak'd the echoes of the mountain, dy'd.
Nor did his grim affociate 'fcape my arm ;
Thy fervant flew the lion and the bear,
I kill'd them both, and bore their fhaggy fpoils

In triumph home.   And shall I fear to meet
Th' uncircumcis'd Philistine? No: that GOD,
Who fav'd me from the bear's destructive fang,.
And hungry lion's jaw, will not he save me
From this Idolater?

SAUL.

           He will, he will!
Go, noble youth! be valiant, and be blefs'd!
The GOD thou ferv'ft will shield thee in the fight,
And nerve thy arm with more than mortal strength.

ABNER.

So the bold Nazarite * a lion flew,
An earneft of his victories o'er Philiftia.

SAUL.

Go, Abner! fee the youth be well equipp'd
With shield and fpear.   Be it thy care to grace him
With all the fit accoutrements of war.
The choiceft mail from my rich armoury take,.
And gird upon his thigh my own try'd fword,
Of nobleft temper'd fteel.

ABNER.

        I shall obey..

DAVID.

Pardon, O king! the coat of plaited mail,
Thefe limbs have never known;. it wou'd not shield,
                        'Twou'd

---

* Samfon. See Judges, chap. xiv.

'Twou'd but encumber one, who never felt
The weight of armour.

SAUL.

　　　　Take thy wish, my son.
Thy sword then, and the GOD of Jacob Guard thee!

DAVID AND GOLIATH.

PART IV.

SCENE, another Part of the Camp.

DAVID.

ETERNAL Justice! in whose awful scale
Th' event of battle hangs! Eternal Mercy,
Whose universal beam illumines all!
If, by thy attributes I may, unblam'd,
Address thee; Lord of glory, hear me now!
O teach these hands to war, these arms to fight!
Thou ever present help in time of need!
Let thy broad mercy, as a shield, defend;

　　　　　　　　　　And

And let thine everlasting arms support me!
Then, tho' the heathen rage, I shall not fear.
JEHOVAH! be my buckler. Mighty LORD!
Thou, who hast deign'd by humble instruments,
To manifest the marvels of thy might,
Be present with me now! 'tis thy own cause!
Thy wisdom will foresee, thy goodness chuse,
And thy omnipotence will execute
Thy high designs, tho' by a feeble arm!
I feel a secret impulse drive me on,
And my soul springs impatient for the fight.
'Tis not the heated spirits, or warm blood
Of sanguine youth; and yet I pant, I burn
To meet th' insulting foe. I thirst for glory;
Yet not the fading glory of renown,
The perishable praise of mortal man.

DAVID, ELIAB, ISRAELITES.

ELIAB.
What do I hear, thou truant? thou hast dar'd,
Ev'n to the awful presence of the king,
Bear thy presumption!

DAVID.
                    He, who fears the LORD,
Shall boldly stand before the face of kings,
And shall not be asham'd.

ELIAB.
                    But what wild dream
Has urg'd thee to this deed of desp'rate rashness?

                                        Their

Thou mean'ſt, ſo have I learn'd, to meet Goliath,
His ſingle arm to thine.

DAVID.

     'Tis what I mean,
Ev'n on this ſpot; each moment I expect
His wiſh'd approach.

ELIAB.

    Go home; return, for ſhame?
Nor madly pull deſtruction on thy head.
Thy doating father, when thy ſhepherd's coat,
Drench'd in thy blood is brought him, will lament,
And rend his furrow'd cheek, and ſilver hair,
As if ſome mighty loſs had touch'd his age;
And mourn, even as the partial patriarch mourn'd,
When Joſeph's bloody garment he receiv'd,
From his leſs dear, not leſs deſerving, ſons.
But whence that glitt'ring ornament, which hangs
Uſeleſs upon thy thigh?

DAIVD.

     'Tis the king's gift.
But thou art right; it ſuits not me, my brother.
Nor ſword I mean to wear, nor ſpear to poize,
Leſt men ſhou'd ſay I put my truſt in ought,
Save an eternal ſhield.

ELIAB.

    Then thou indeed
Art bent to ſeek thy death.

DAVID.

    And what is death?
Is it ſo terrible to die, my brother?

Or

Or grant it terrible, fay is it not
Inevitable too? If, by eluding death,
When fome high duty calls us forth to die,
We cou'd for ever fhun it, and efcape
The univerfal lot; then fond felf-love,
Then human prudence, boldly might produce
Their fine-fpun arguments, their learn'd harangues,
Their cobweb arts, their phrafe fophiftical,
Their fubtile doubts, and all the fpecious trick,
Of eloquent cunning lab'ring for its end.
But fince, howe'er protracted, death will come,
Why fondly ftudy, with ingenious pains,
To put it off?——To breathe a little longer,
Is to defer our fate, but not to fhun it:
Small gain! which Wifdom with indiff'rent eye
Beholds.   Why wifh to drink the bitter dregs
Of life's exhaufted chalice, whofe laft runnings,
Ev'n at the beft, are vapid? Why not die,
(If Heav'n fo will) in manhood's op'ning bloom,
When all the flufh of life is gay about us,
When fprightly youth, with many a new-born joy,
Solicits every fenfe? So may we then
Prefent a facrifice, unmeet, indeed,
(Ah, how unmeet!) but more acceptable
Than the world's leavings; than a worn-out heart,
By vice enfeebled, and by vain defires
Sunk and exhaufted!

                    E L I A B.
                    Hark! I hear a found
Of multitudes approaching!

                              DAVID.

DAVID.

'Tis the giant!
I fee him not, but hear his meafur'd pace.

ELIAB.

Look, where his pond'rous fhield is borne before him!

DAVID.

Like a broad moon its ample difk protends.
But foft, what unknown prodigy appears?
A moving mountain cas'd in polifh'd brafs!

ELIAB. [*Getting behind* DAVID.]

How's this? thou doft not tremble. Thy firm joints
Betray no fear: Thy accents are not broken:
Thy cheek retains its red, thine eye its luftre.
He comes more near. Doft thou not fear him now?

DAVID.

No.
The vaft coloffal ftatue nor infpires
Refpect nor fear. Mere magnitude of form,
Without proportion'd intellect and valour,
Strikes not my foul with rev'rence nor with awe.

ELIAB.

Near, and more near, he comes. I hold it rafh
To ftay fo near him, and expofe a life,
Which may hereafter ferve the ftate. Farewell!
[*Exit.*

[GOLIATH *advances, clad in complete armour. One bear-
ing his fhield precedes him. The oppofing armies are feen
at a diftance, drawn up on each fide of the valley.*
GOLIATH *begins to fpeak, before he comes on.* DAVID
ftands in the fame place, with an air of indifference.]

K   GOLI-

GOLIATH.

Where is the mighty man of war, who dares
Accept the challenge of Philiftia's chief?
What victor-king, what gen'ral drench'd in blood,
Claims this high privilege? What are his rights?
What proud credentials does the boafter bring,
To prove his claim! What cities laid in afhes?
What ruin'd provinces? What flaughter'd realms?
What heads of heroes, and what hearts of kings,
In battle kill'd, or at his altars flain,
Has he to boaft? Is his bright armoury
Thick fet with fpears, and fwords, and coats of mail,
Of vanquifh'd nations, by his fingle arm
Subdued? Where is the mortal man fo bold,
So much a wretch, fo out of love with life,
To dare the weight of this uplifted fpear,
Which never fell innoxious? Yet I fwear,
I grudge the glory to his parting foul
To fall by this right-hand. 'Twill fweeten death,
To know he had the honour to contend
With the dread fon of Anak. Lateft time
From blank oblivion fhall retrieve *his* name,
Who dar'd to perifh in unequal fight
With Gath's triumphant champion. Come, advance!
Philiftia's Gods to Ifrael's. Sound, my herald—
Sound for the battle ftrait!

[Herald founds the trumpet.

DAVID.

Behold thy foe!

GOLIATH.

I fee him not.

DAVID.

DAVID.
Behold hm here !

GOLIATH.
Say, where ?
Direct my fight. I do not war with boys.

DAVID.
I ftand prepar'd, thy fingle arm to mine.

GOLIATH.
Why, this is mockery, Minion ! it may chance
To coft thee dear. Sport not with things above thee :
But tell me who, of all this num'rous hoft,
Expects his death from me ? Which is the man,
Whom Ifrael fends to meet my bold defiance ?

DAVID.
Th' election of my fov'reign falls on me.

GOLIATH.
On thee ! on thee ! by Dagon 'tis too much !
Thou curled Minion ! thou a nation's champion !.
'Twou'd move my mirth at any other time ;
But trifling's out of tune. Begone, light boy !
And tempt me not too far.

DAVID.
I do defy thee ;
Thou foul idolater ! haft thou not fcorn'd
The armies of the living God I ferve ?
By me he will avenge upon thy head
Thy nation's fin's and thine. Arm'd with his name,

Un-

Unſhrinking, I dare meet the ſtouteſt foe
That ever bath'd his hoſtile ſpear in blood.

GOLIATH, *ironically.*

Indeed! 'tis wond'rous well! Now, by my Gods,
The ſtripling plays the orator! Vain boy!
Keep cloſe to that ſame bloodleſs war of words,
And thou ſhalt ſtill be ſafe.   Tongue-valiant warrior!
Where is thy ſylvan crook, with garlands hung,
Of idle field-flowers? Where thy wanton harp,
Thou dainty-finger'd hero? better ſtrike
Its note laſcivious, or the lulling lute
Touch ſoftly, than provoke the trumpet's rage.
I will not ſtain the honour of my ſpear
With thy inglorious blood.   Shall that fair cheek
Be ſcarr'd with wounds unſeemly? Rather go,
And hold fond dalliance with the Syrian maids;
To wanton meaſures dance, and let them braid
The bright luxuriance of thy golden hair;
They, for their loſt Adonis, may miſtake
Thy dainty form.

DAVID.

Peace, thou unhallow'd railer!
O tell it not in Gath, nor let the ſound
Reach Aſkelon, how once your ſlaughter'd Lords,
By mighty * Samſon found one common grave:
When his broad ſhoulder the firm pillars heav'd,
And to its baſe the tott'ring fabric ſhook.

GOLIATH.

---

* *Judges,* chap. xvi.

GOLIATH.

Infulting boy! perhaps thou haft not hear'd
The infamy of that inglorious day,
When your weak hofts at * Eben-ezer pitch'd
Their quick-abandon'd tents? Then; when your ark,
Your talifman, your charm, your boafted pledge
Of fafety and fuccefs, was tamely loft!
And yet not tamely, fince by me 'twas won.
When with this good right-arm I thinn'd your ranks,
And bravely crufh'd, beneath a fingle blow,
The chofen guardians of this vaunted fhrine,
Hophni † and Phineas. The fam'd ark itfelf,
I bore to Afhdod.

DAVID.

I remember too,
Since thou provok'ft th' unwelcome truth, how all
Your blufhing priefts beheld their idols fhame;
When proftrate Dagon fell before the ark,
And your frail God was fhiver'd. Then Philiftia,
Idolatrous Philiftia flew for fuccour
To Ifrael's help, and all her fmitten nobles
Confefs'd the LORD was GOD, and the blefs'd ark,
Gladly, with reverential awe reftor'd!

GOLIATH.

By Afhdod's fane thou ly'ft. Now will I meet thee,
Thou infect warrior! fince thou dar'ft me thus!

Already

---

* 1 Samuel, chap. v.

† Commentators fay, that the Chaldee Paraphrafe makes
Goliath boaft, that he had killed Hophni, and Phineas, and
taken the ark prifoner.

Already I behold thy mangled limbs,
Diſſever'd each from each, ere long to feed
The fierce, blood-ſnuffing vulture.   Mark me well!
Around my ſpear I'll twiſt thy ſhining locks,
And toſs in air thy head all gaſh'd with wounds ;
Thy lips, yet quiv'ring with the dire convulſion
Of recent death! Art thou not terrified?

DAVID.
No.

True courage is not mov'd by breath of words.
But the raſh bravery of boiling blood,
Impetuous, knows no ſettled principle.
A fev'riſh tide, it has its ebbs and flows,
As ſpirits riſe or fall, as wine inflames,
Or circumſtances change.   But inborn courage;
The gen'rous child of Fortitude and Faith,
Holds its firm empire in the conſtant ſoul ;
And, like the ſtedfaſt pole-ſtar, never once
From the ſame fix'd and faithful point declines.

GOLIATH.

The curſes of Philiſtia's gods be on thee !
This fine-drawn ſpeech is meant to lengthen out
That little life thy words pretend to ſcorn.

DAVID.

Ha! ſay'ſt thou ſo? come on then! Mark us well.
Thou com'ſt to me with ſword, and ſpear, and ſhield !
In the dread name of Iſrael's GOD, I come ;
The living LORD of HOSTS, whom thou defy'ſt !
Yet tho' no ſhield I bring, no arms, except
Theſe five ſmooth ſtones I gather'd from the brook,

With

With fuch a fimple fling as fhepherds ufe ;
Yet all expos'd, defencelefs as I am,
The GOD I ferve fhall give thee up a prey
To my victorious arm.   This day, I mean
To make th' uncircumcifed tribes confefs
There is a GOD in Ifrael.   I will give thee,
Spite of thy vaunted ftrength, and giant bulk,
To glut the carrion kites.   Nor thee alone ;
The mangled carcafes of your thick hofts,
Shall fpread the plains of Elah : till Philiftia,
Thro' all her trembling tents and flying bands,
Shall own that Judah's GOD is GOD indeed !
I dare thee to the trial !

GOLIATH.
                    Follow me.
In this good fpear I truft.

DAVID.
                    I truft in Heaven !
The GOD of battles ftimulates my arm,
And fires my foul with ardor, not its own.

                              DAVID.

DAVID AND GOLIATH.

PART V.

SCENE, The Tent of SAUL.

SAUL, *rifing from his Couch.*

OH! that I knew the black and midnight arts
Of wizard forcery! that I cou'd call
The flumb'ring fpirit from the fhades of hell!
Or, like Chaldean fages, cou'd foreknow
Th' event of things unacted! I might then
Anticipate my fortune.   How I'm fall'n!
The fport of vain chimeras, the weak flave
Of Fear, and fickly Fancy; coveting
To know the arts, which foul diviners ufe.
Thick blood, and moping melancholy, lead
To baleful Superftition; that fell fiend,
Whofe with'ring charms blaft the fair bloom of virtue.
Why did my wounded pride with fcorn reject
The wholefome truths, which holy Samuel told me?
Why drive him from my prefence? he might now
Raife my funk foul, and my benighted mind

Enlighten

Enlighten with religion's cheering ray.
He dar'd to menace me with lofs of empire;
And I, for that bold honefty, difmifs'd him.
" Another fhall poffefs thy throne, he cry'd,
" A ftranger!" This unwelcome prophecy
Has lin'd my crown, and ftrew'd my couch, with thorns,
Each ray of op'ning merit I difcern
In friend or foe, diftracts my troubled foul,
Left he fhou'd prove my rival. But this morn,
Ev'n my young champion, lovely as he look'd
In blooming valour, ftruck me to the foul,
With jealoufy's barb'd dart. O Jealoufy!
Thou uglieft fiend of hell!, thy deadly venom
Preys on my vitals, turns the healthful hue
Of my frefh cheek to haggard fallownefs,
And drinks my fpirit up!

[*A flourifh of trumpets, fhouting, &c. &c.*

What founds are thofe?
The combat is decided. Hark! again,
Thofe fhouts proclaim it! Now, O GOD of JACOB,
If yet thou haft not quite withdrawn from Saul
Thy light and favour, profper me this once!
But Abner comes! I dread to hear his tale.
Fair Hope, with fmiling face, but ling'ring foot,
Has long deceiv'd me.

ABNER.
King of Ifrael, hail!
Now thou art king indeed. The youth has conquer'd,
Goliath's dead.

SAUL.
Oh, fpeak thy tale again,
Left my fond ears deceive me!

L   ABNER.

ABNER.

Thy young champion
, Has flain the giant.

SAUL.

Then God is gracious ftill,
In fpite of my offences! But, good Abner,
How was it? tell me all! Where is my champion?
Q—ck let me prefs him to my grateful heart,
And pay him a king's thanks. And yet, who knows?
This forward friend may prove an active foe.
No more of that.—Tell me the whole, brave Abner!
And paint the glorious acts of my young heroe!

ABNER.

Full in the centre of the camp they ftood;
Th' oppofing armies rang'd on either fide,
In proud array. The haughty giant ftalk'd,
Stately, acrofs the valley. Next the youth,
With modeft confidence advanc'd. Nor pomp,
Nor gay parade, nor martial ornament,
His graceful form adorn'd. Goliath ftrait,
With folemn ftate, began the bufy work
Of dreadful preparation. In one place,
His clofely jointed mail an op'ning left,
For air, and only one : the watchful youth
Mark'd that the beaver of his helm was up.
Meanwhile the Giant fuch a blow devis'd,
As wou'd have crufh'd him ; this the youth perceiv'd,
And from his well directed fling, he hurl'd,
With dextrous aim, a ftone, which funk, deep lodg'd,
In the capacious forehead of the foe.
Then with a cry, as loud and terrible,
As Lybian lions roaring for their young,

Quite

Quite ftunn'd, the furious Giant ftagger'd, reel'd,
And fell : the mighty mafs of man fell prone.
With its own weight his fhatter'd bulk was bruis'd.
His clattering arms rung dreadful thro' the field,
And the firm bafis of the folid earth
Shook. Chok'd with blood and duft, he curs'd his gods,
And dy'd blafpheming ! Strait the victor youth
Drew from its fheath the Giant's pond'rous fword,
And from th' enormous trunk, the goary head,
Furious in death, he fever'd. The grim vifage
Look'd threat'ning ftill, and ftill frown'd horribly.

SAUL.
O glorious deed ! O valiant conqueror !

ABNER.
The youth fo calm appear'd, fo nobly firm ;
So cool, yet fo intrepid ; that thefe eyes
Ne'er faw fuch temperate valour, fo chaftis'd
By modefty.

SAUL.
Thou dwell'ft upon his praife
With needlefs circumftance. 'Twas nobly done ,
But others too have fought !

ABNER.
None, none fo bravely

SAUL.
What follow'd next ?

L 2   ABNER.

ABNER.

The shouting Israelites
On the Philistines rush'd, and still pursue
Their routed remnan's. In dismay, their bands,
Disorder'd fly. While shouts of loud acclaim
Pursue their brave deliverer. Lo, he comes!·
Bearing the Giant's head, and shining sword,
His well-earn'd trophies.

SAUL, ABNER, DAVID.

[DAVID, *bearing* GOLIATH's *head and sword. He kneels,
and lays both at* SAUL's *feet.*] ·

SAUL.

Welcome to my heart,
My glorious champion! my deliverer, welcome!
How shall I speak the swelling gratitude
Of my full heart? or give thee the high praise
Thy gallant deeds deserve?

DAVID.

O mighty king!
Sweet is the breath of praise, when giv'n by those.
Whose own high merit claims the praise they give.
But let not this one fortunate event,
By Heav'n directed, be ascrib'd to me.
I might have fought with equal skill and courage,
And not have gain'd this conquest; then had shame,
Harsh obloquy, and foul disgrace befal'n me.
But prosp'rous fortune gains the praise of valour.

SAUL.

I like not this. In every thing superior!
He soars above me. *(Aside.)* Modest youth, thou'rt right.
And

And fortune, as thou fay'ft, deferves the praife
We give to human valour.

DAVID.
Rather fay,
The GOD OF HOSTS deferves it.

SAUL.
Tell me, youth !
What is thy name, and what thy father's houfe ?

DAVID.
My name is David, Jeffe is my fire,
An humble Bethlemite of Judah's tribe.

SAUL.
David, the fon of Jeffe ! Sure that name
Has been familiar to me ! Nay, thy voice,
Thy form and features, I remember too,
Tho, faint, and indiftinctly.

ABNER.
In this Hero
Behold thy fweet mufician ; he, whofe harp
Expell'd the melancholy fiend, whofe pow'r
Enfiav'd thy fpirit.

SAUL.
This the modeft youth,
Whom, for his fkill and virtues, I preferr'd
To bear my armour ?

DAVID.
I am he, O king !

SAUL.

SAUL.

Why this concealment? tell me, valiant David!
Why didft thou hide thy birth and name till now?

DAVID.

O king! I wou'd not ought from favour claim,
Or on remember'd fervices prefume:
But on the ftrength of my own actions ftand,
Ungrac'd and unfupported.

ABNER.

Well he merits
The honours, which await him. Why, O king!
Doft thou delay to blefs his doubting heart
With his well earn'd rewards? Thy lovely daughter,
By right of conqueft his!

SAUL, *to* DAVID.

True—thou haft won her.
She fhall be thine—Yes, a king's word is paft.

DAVID.

O boundlefs blefling! What, fhall fhe be mine,
For whom contending monarchs might renounce
Their flighted crowns?

[*Sounds of mufical inftruments heard at a diftance.
Shouting and finging. A grand proceffion.* CHO-
RUS *of* HEBREW WOMEN.]

SAUL.

How's this? what founds of joy
Salute my ears? what means this pageantry?

This

This merry found of tabret and of harp?.
What mean thefe idle inftruments of triumph?
Thefe women, who in fair proceffion move,
Making fweet melody?

ABNER.
                    To pay due honour
To David, are they come.

SAUL.   [*Afide.*
                    A rival's praife
Is difcord to the ear of jealoufy!

[*Martial fymphony.   After which* CHORUS *of* WO-
    MEN *fing.*]

I.
PREPARE! your feftal rites prepare!
Let your triumphs rend the air!
Idol gods fhall reign no more,
We the living LORD adore!
Let heathen hofts on human helps repofe,
Since Ifrael's GOD has routed Ifrael's foes.

II.
Let remoteft nations know,
Proud Goliath's overthrow:
Fall'n, Philiftia! is thy truft,
Dagon's honour laid in duft!
Who fears the LORD of Glory, need not fear
The brazen armour, or the lifted fpear.

III.
See the routed fquadrons fly!
Hark! their clamours rend the fky!

                                        Blood

Blood and carnage ſtain the field!
See, the vanquiſh'd nations yield!
Diſmay and terror fill the frighten'd land;
While conq'ring David routs the trembling band.

IV.

Lo! upon the tented field,
Royal Saul has thouſands kill'd!
Lo! upon th' enſanguin'd plain,
David has ten thouſands ſlain!
Let mighty Saul his vanquiſh'd thouſands tell,
While tenfold triumphs David's victories ſwell.

THE END.

PERSONS of the DRAMA.

BELSHAZZAR, King of Babylon.
NITOCRIS, the Queen-mother.
COURTIERS, ASTROLOGERS, PARASITES.
DANIEL, the JEWISH Prophet.
Captive JEWS, &c. &c.

SCENE, BABYLON. Time, Night.

☞ The Subject of this Drama is taken from the Fifth
Chapter of the Prophet DANIEL.

M

BELSHAZZAR:

A

SACRED DRAMA.

PART I.

How art thou fallen from Heaven, O Lucifer, Son of the
Morning! How art thou cut down to the ground, who
didſt weaken the nations!

ISAIAH.

SCENE, near the Palace of BABYLON.

DANIEL, *and captive* JEWS.

DANIEL.

PARENT of life and light! ſole ſource of good!
Whoſe tender mercies thro' the tide of time,
In long ſucceſſive order, have ſuſtain'd,
And ſav'd the ſons of Iſrael! Thou, whoſe pow'r
Deliver'd righteous Noah from the flood,
The whelming flood, the grave of human kind!

Oh

Oh Thou! whofe guardian care, and out-ftretch'd hand,
Refcu'd young Ifaac from the lifted arm,
Rais'd, at thy bidding, to devote a fon,
An only fon, doom'd by his fire to die.
(Oh, faving Faith, by fuch obedience prov'd!
Oh bleft Obedience, hallow'd this by faith!)
Thou, who in mercy favd'ft the chofen race,
In the wild defert; and didft there fuftain them,
By wonder-working love, tho' they rebell'd,
And murmur'd at the miracles that fav'd them!
Oh, hear thy fervant Daniel! hear, and help!
Thou! whofe almighty pow'r did after raife
Succeffive leaders to defend our race:
Who fenteft vailant Jofhua to the field,
Thy people's champion, to the conq'ring field;
Where the revolving planet of the night,
Sufpended in her radiant round, was ftay'd;
And the bright fun, arrefted in his courfe,
Stupenduoufly ftood ftill!

CHORUS of JEWS.

I.

What aileth thee, that thou ftood'ft ftill,
O fun! nor did thy flaming orb decline?
And thou, O moon! in Ajalon's dark vale,
Why did'ft thou long beyond thy period fhine?

II.

Was it at Jofhua's dread command,
The leader of the Ifraelitifh band?
Yes——at a mortal bidding both ftood ftill;
'Twas Jofhua's word, but 'twas JEHOVAH's will.

III.

What all-controuling hand had force
▊ ▊ eternal Nature's conftant courfe?
The ▊ d'ring moon to one fix'd fpo. confine,
But ▊ ▊, whofe fiat bade the planets fhine?

DANIEL.

O Thou! who, when thy difcontented hoft,
Tir'd of JEHOVAH's rule, defir'd a king,
In anger gav'ft them Saul; and then again
Didft wreft the regal fceptre from his hand,
To give it David—David, beft belov'd!
Illuftrious David! Poet, prophet, king!
Thou, who didft fuffer Solomon his fon,
To build a glorious temple to thy name!
Oh hear thy fervants, and forgive them too,
If, by fevere neceffity compell'd,
We worfhip here—We have no temple now;
Altar or fanctuary, none is left.

CHORUS of JEWS.

O Judah! let thy captive fons deplore,
Thy far-fam'd temple's now no more!
Fall'n is thy facred fane, thy glory gone,
Fall'n is thy temple, Solomon.

Ne'er did Barbaric kings behold,
With all their fhining gems, their burnifh'd gold,
A fane fo perfect, bright and fair;
For GOD himfelf was wont t'inhabit there:
Between the Cherubim his glory ftood,
While the high-prieft alone the dazzling fplender view'd.

How

How fondly did the Tyrian artift ftrive,
    His name to lateft time fhould live!
Such wealth the ftranger wonder'd to behold :
Gold were the tablets, and the vafes gold.
    Of cedar fuch an ample ftore,
Exhaufted Lebanon could yield no more.
Bending before the Ruler of the fky,
    Well might the royal founder cry,
Fill'd with an holy dread, a rev'rend fear,
Will God in very deed inhabit here ?
    The heav'n of heav'ns beneath his feet,
Is for the bright inhabitant unmeet :
Archangels proftrate wait his high commands,
And will he deign to dwell in temples made with hands ?

DANIEL.

Yes, thou art ever prefent, Pow'r fupreme !
Not circumfcrib'd by time, nor fix'd to fpace,
Confin'd to altars, nor to temples bound.
In wealth, in want, in freedom, or in chains,
In dungeons or on thrones, the faithful find thee !
Ev'n in the burning cauldron thou waft near
To Shadrach and the holy brotherhood ;
The unhurt martyrs blefs'd thee in the flames ;
They fought, and found thee, call'd, and thou waft there.

Firft JEW.

How chang'd our ftate ! Judah ! thy glory's fall'n ;
Thy joys for hard captivity exchang'd ;
And thy fad fons breathe the polluted air
Of Babylon, where deities obfcene
Infult the living God ; and to his fervants,

                                    The

The priests of wretched idols, made with hands,
Shew contumelious scorn.

DANIEL.
> 'Tis Heav'n's high will.

Second JEW.

If I forget thee, O Jerusalem!
If I not fondly cherish thy lov'd image,
Ev'n in the giddy hour of thoughtless mirth;
If I not rather view thy prostrate walls
Than haughty Babylon's imperial tow'rs;
Then may my tongue refuse to frame the strains
Of sweetest harmony; my rude right hand
Forget, with sounds symphonious, to accord
The harp of Jesse's son, to Sion's songs.

First JEW.

Oft, on Euphrates' ever verdant banks,
Where drooping willows form a mournful shade;
With all the pride which prosp'rous fortunes give,
And all th' unfeeling mirth of happy men,
Th' insulting Babylonians ask a song;
Such songs as erst, in better days, were sung
By Korah's sons, or heav'n-taught Asaph set
To loftiest measures; then our bursting hearts
Feel all their woes afresh; the galling chain
Of bondage crushes then the free-born soul
With wringing anguish; from the trembling lip
Th' unfinish'd cadence falls, and the big tear,
While it relieves, betrays the woe-fraught soul.
For who can view Euphrates' pleasant stream,
Its drooping willows, and its verdant banks,

And not to wounded memory recal
The piny groves of fertile Palæftine,
The vales of Solyma, and Jordan's ftream?

DANIEL.

Firm faith, and deep fubmiffion to high Heav'n,
Will teach us to endure, without a murmur,
What feems fo hard. Think what the holy hoft
Of patriarchs, faints, and prophets, have fuftain'd
In the bleft caufe of Truth! And fhall not we,
O men of Judah! dare what thefe have dar'd,
And boldly pafs thro' the refining fire
Of fierce affliction? Yes, be witnefs, Heav'n!
Old as I am, I will not fhrink at death,
Come in what fhape it may, if GOD fo will,
By peril to confirm and prove my faith.
Oh! I wou'd dare yon' den of hungry lions,
Rather than paufe to fill the tafk affign'd,
By wifdom infinite. Nor think I boaft,
Not in myfelf, but in thy ftrength I truft,
Spirit of GOD!

Firft JEW.

Prophet! thy words fupport,
And raife our finking fouls.

DANIEL.

Behold yon' palace,
Where proud Belfhazzar keeps his wanton court!
I knew it once beneath another lord,
His grandfire *, who fubdued Jehoiachin,

And

---

* Nebucbadnezzar.

And hither brought fad Judah's captive tribes ;
Together with the rich and facred relics
Of our fam'd temple ; all the holy treafure,
The golden vafes, and the facred cups,
Which grac'd, in happier times, the fanctuary.

Second J E W.

May 'He, to whofe bleft ufe they were devoted,
Preferve them from pollution ; and once more,
In his own gracious time, reftore the temple !

D A N I E L.

I, with fome favour'd youths of Jewifh race,
Was lodg'd in his own palace, and inftructed
In all the various learning of the eaft :
But HE, on whofe great name our fathers call'd,
Preferv'd us from the perils of a court ;
And warn'd us to avoid the tempting cates
Pernicious lux'ry offer'd to our tafte.
Fell luxury ! more perilous to youth
Than ftorms or quickfands, poverty or chains.

Second J E W.

He, who can guard 'gainft the low baits of fenfe,
Will find Temptation's arrows hurtlefs ftrike
Againft the brazen fhield of Temperance.
For 'tis th' inferior appetites enthrall
The man, and quench th' immortal light within him ;
The fenfes take the foul an eafy prey,
And fink th' imprifon'd fpirit into brute.

DANIEL.

Twice *, by the fpirit of GOD, did I expound
The vifions of the king; his foul was touch'd,
And twice did he repent, and proftrate fall
Before the GOD of Daniel : yet again,
Pow'r, flatt'ry, and profperity, undid him.
When from the lofty ramparts of his palace,
He view'd the fplendors of the royal city,
That magazine of wealth, which proud Euphrates
Wafts from each diftant corner of the earth;
When he beheld the adamantine towers,
The brazen gates, the bulwarks of his ftrength,
The pendent gardens, art's ftupendous work,
The wonder of the world!—The proud Chaldean,
Mad with the infolence of boundlefs wealth,
And pow'r fupreme, conceiv'd himfelf a God.
" This mighty Babylon is mine," he cried,
" My wondrous pow'r, my godlike arm atchiev'd it.
" I fcorn fubmiffion, own no deity
" Above my own."—While the blafphemer fpoke,
The wrath of Heav'n inflicted inftant vengeance;
Stripp'd him of that bright reafon he abus'd,
And drove him from the chearful haunts of men,
A naked, wretched, helplefs, fenfelefs thing;
Companion of the brutes, his equals now.

Firft JEW.

Nor does his impious grandfon, proud Belfhazzar,
Fall fhort of his offences; nay, he wants
The valiant fpirit, and the active foul,

N   Of

---

* Daniel, chap. ii. and iv.

Of his progenitor: for Pleafure's flave,
Though bound in flow'ry fetters, filky-foft,
Is more fubdued, than is the cafual victim
Of furious rage, and violent ambition.
Ambition is a fierce, but fhort-liv'd fire;
But Pleafure with a conftant flame confumes.
War flays her thoufands; but deftructive pleafure,
More fell, more fatal, her ten thoufands flays:
The young, luxurious king fhe fondly wooes
In every fhape of am'rous blandifhment;
With adulation fmooth enfnares his foul,
With love betrays him, and with wine inflames.
She ftrews her magic poppies o'er his couch;
And with del'cious opiates charms him down,
In fatal flumbers bound. Though Babylon
Is now invefted by the warlike troops
Of the young Cyrus, Perfia's valiant prince;
Who, in conjunction with the Median king,
Darius, fam'd for conqueft, now prepares
To ftorm the city: not th' impending horrors
Which ever wait a fiege, have power to wake
To thought, or fenfe, th' intoxicated king.

DANIEL.

Ev'n in this night of univerfal dread,
A mighty army threat'ning at the gates;
This very night, as if in fcorn of danger,
The diffolute Belfhazzar holds a feaft
Magnificently impious, meant to honour
Belus, the fav'rite Babylonifh idol.
Lewd parafites compofe his wanton court,
Whofe impious flatt'ries footh his monftrous crimes:
They juftify his vices, and extol

His

His boaftful phrafe, as if he were fome god.
Whate'er he fays, they fay; what he commands,
Implicitly they do; they echo back
His blafphemies, with fhouts of loud acclaim;
And when he wounds the tortur'd ear of Virtue,
They cry, All hail! Belfhazzar live for ever!
To-night a thoufand nobles fill his hall,
Princes, and all the dames who grace the court;.
All but the virtuous queen, fage Nitocris;
Ah! how unlike the impious king her fon!
She never mingles in the midnight fray,
Nor crowns the guilty banquet with her prefence.
The royal fair is rich in every virtue
Which can adorn the queen, or grace the woman.
But for the wifdom of her prudent counfels
This wretched empire had been long undone.
Not fam'd Semiramis, Affyria's pride,
Cou'd boaft a brighter mind, or firmer foul;
Beneath the gentle reign of * Merodach,
Her royal lord, our nation tafted peace.
Our captive monarch, fad Jehoiachin,
Grown grey in a clofe prifon's horrid gloom,
He freed from bondage; brought the hoary king
To tafte once more the long-forgotten fweets
Of precious liberty, and chearful light;
Pour'd in his wounds the lenient balm of kindnefs,
And blefs'd his fetting hour of life with peace.

[*Sound of trumpets is heard at a diftance.*

Firft JEW.

.That found proclaims the banquet is begun.

N 2   Sfcond

* 2 *Kings, chap.* xxv.

Second JEW.

Hark! the licentious uproar grows more loud.
The vaulted roof refounds with fhouts of mirth,
And the firm palace fhakes! Retire, my friends;
This madnefs is not meet for fober ears.
If any of our race were found fo near,
"Twou'd but expofe us to the rude attack
Of ribaldry obfcene, and impious jefts,
From thefe mad fons of Belial, now inflam'd·
To deeds of riot from the wanton feaft.

DANIEL.

Here part we then! but when again to meet,
Who knows fave Heav'n? Yet, O, my friends! I feel.
An impulfe more than human ftir my breaft.
Rapt in prophetic * vifion I behold
Things hid as yet from mortal fight. I fee
The dart of vengeance tremble in the air,
Ere long to pierce the impious king. Ev'n now
The fierce, deftroying angel ftalks abroad,
And brandifhes aloft the two-edg'd fword
Of retribution keen; he foon will ftrike,
And Babylon fhall weep as Sion wept.
Pafs but a little while, and you fhall fee
This queen of cities proftrate on the earth.
This haughty miftrefs of the kneeling world,
How fhall fhe fit difhonour'd in the duft,
In tarnifh'd pomp and folitary woe!
How fhall fhe fhroud her glories in the dark,
And in opprobrious filence hide her head!

Lament,

---

* See the Prophecies of Ifaiah, chap. xlvii. and others

Lament, O virgin daughter of Chaldea!
For thou fhalt fall, imperial queen! fhalt fall!
No more Sidonian robes fhall grace thy limbs.
To purple garments, fackcloth fhall fucceed;
And fordid duft and afhes fhall fupply
The od'rous nard and caffia. Thou, who faid'ft,
I am, and there is none befide me: thou,
Ev'n thou, imperial Babylon! fhalt fall:
Thy glory quite eclips'd! The pleafant found
Of viol, and of harp, fhall charm no more;
Nor fong of Syrian damfels fhall be heard,
Refponfive to the lute's luxurious note.
But the loud bittern's cry, the raven's croak,
The bat's fell fcream, the lonely owl's dull plaint,
And every hideous bird with ominous fhriek,
Shall fcare affrighted Silence from thy walls.
While DESOLATION, fnatching from the hand
Of time the fcythe of ruin, fits aloft,
In dreadful majefty and horrid pomp;
Glancing with fullen pride thy crumbling tow'rs,
Thy broken battlements, thy columns fall'n:
Then, pointing to the mifchiefs fhe has made,
The fiend exclaims, This once was Babylon!

BELSHAZZAR.

PART II.

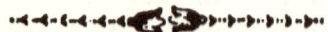

SCENE, *The Court of* BELSHAZZAR. *The King seated on a magnificent throne. Princes, Nobles, and Attendants. Ladies of the Court. Music... A supberb Banquet.*

First COURTIER. *Rises, and kneels.*

Hail, mighty king!

Second COURTIER.
Belshazzar, live for ever!

Third COURTIER.
Sun of the world, and light of kings, all hail!

Fourth COURTIER.
With lowest reverence, such as best becomes
The humblest creatures of imperial power,
Behold a thousand nobles bend before thee!

Princes

Princes far fam'd, and dames of high defcent :
Yet all this pride of wealth, this boaft of beauty,
Shrinks into nought before thine awful eye;
And lives, or dies, as the king frowns, or fmiles!

BELSHAZZAR.

This is fuch homage, as becomes your love;
And fuits the mighty monarch of mankind.

Fifth COURTIER.

The bending world fhou'd proftrate thus before thee;
And pay, not only praife, but adoration!

BELSHAZZAR. *Rifes, and comes forward.*

Let dull philofophy preach felf-denial;
Let envious poverty, and fnarling age,
Proudly declaim againft the joys they know not.
Let the deluded Jews, who fondly hope
Some fancied heav'n hereafter, mortify;
And lofe the actual bleffings of this world,
To purchafe others which may never come.
Our Gods may promife lefs, but give us more.
Ill cou'd my ardent fpirit be content
With meagre abftinence, and hungry hope.
Let thofe, misjudging Ifraelites, who want
The nimble fpirits, and the active foul,
Call their blunt feelings virtue: let them drudge,
In regular progreffion, thro' the round
Of formal duty, and of daily toil;
And, when they want the genius to be bleft,
Believe their harfh aufterity is goodnefs.
If there be Gods, they meant we fhou'd be happy;
Why give us elfe thefe appetites to be for

And

And why, the means to crown them with indulgence?
To burſt the feeble bonds, which hold the vulgar,
Is noble daring.

Firſt C O U R T I E R.
And is therefore worthy
The high imperial ſpirit of Belſhazzar.

Second C O U R T I E R.
Behold a banquet, which the gods might ſhare.

B E L S H A Z Z A R.
To-night, my friends! your monarch ſhall be bleſt
With ev'ry various joy; to night is ours;
Nor ſhall the envious gods, who view our bliſs,
And ſicken as they view, to-night diſturb us.
Bring all the richeſt ſpices of the Eaſt,
The od'rous caſſia, and the dropping myrrh;
The liquid amber, and the fragrant gums;
Rob Gilead ot its balms, Belſhazzar bids,
And leave the Arabian groves without an odour.
Bring freſheſt flow'rs, exhauſt the blooming ſpring,
Twine the green myrtle with the ſhort-liv'd roſe;
And ever, as the bluſhing garland fades,
We'll learn to ſnatch the fugitive delight,
And graſp the flying joy ere it eſcape us.
Come—fill the ſmiling goblet for the king;
Belſhazzar will not let a moment paſs,
Unmark'd by ſome enjoyment! The full bowl
Let every gueſt partake!
             [*Courtiers kneel, and drink.*

Firſt COURTIER.

Here's to the king!
Light of the world, and glory of the earth,
Whoſe word is fate!

BELSHAZZAR.

Yes, we are likeſt gods,
When we have pow'r, and uſe it. What is wealth,
But the bleſt means to gratify deſire?
I will not have a wiſh, a hope, a thought,
That ſhall not know fruition. What is empire?
The privilege to puniſh and enjoy;
To feel our pow'r in making others fear it;
To taſte of pleaſure's cup till we grow giddy,
And think ourſelves immortal. This is empire!
My anceſtors ſcarce taſted of its joys:
Shut from the ſprightly world, and all its charms,
In cumbrous majeſty, in ſullen ſtate,
And dull unſocial dignity they liv'd;
Far from the ſight of an admiring world,
That world, whoſe gaze makes half the charms of greatneſs;
They nothing knew of empire but the name,
Or ſaw it in the looks of trembling ſlaves;
And all they felt of royalty was care.
But I will ſee, and know it of myſelf;
Youth, wealth, and greatneſs court me to be bleſt,
And Pow'r and Pleaſure, draw with equal force
And ſweet attraction: both I will embrace
With fond delight; but this is Pleaſure's day;
Ambition will have time to reign hereafter;
It is the proper appetite of age.
The luſt of pow'r ſhall lord it uncontroul'd,
When all the gen'rous feelings grow obtuſe,

O   And

And ftern dominion holds, with rigid hand,
His iron rein, and fits and fways alone.
But youth is Pleafure's hour!

Firft C O U R T I E R.

Perifh the flave
Who, with officious counfel, wou'd oppofe
The king's defire, whofe flighteft wifh is law!

B E L S H A Z Z A R.

Now ftrike the loud-ton'd lyre, and fofter lute;
Let me have mufic, with the nobler aid
Of poefy! Where are thofe cunning men,
Who boaft, by chofen founds, and meafur'd fweetnefs,
To fet the bufy fpirits in a flame,
And cool them at their will? who know the art
To call the hidden pow'rs of numbers forth,
And make that pliant inftrument, the mind,
Yield to the pow'rful fympathy of found,
Obedient to the mafter's artful hand?
Such magic is in fong! Then give me fong;
Yet not at firft fuch foul-diffolving ftrains,
As melt the foften'd fenfe; but fuch bold meafures,
As may inflame my fpirit to defpife
The ambitious Perfian, that prefumptuous boy,
Who rafhly dares ev'n now inveft our city,
And menaces th' invincible Belfhazzar.

A grand CONCERT *of* MUSIC, *after which an* ODE.

In vain fhall Perfian Cyrus dare
With great Belfhazzar wage unequal war:

In vain Darius fhall combine,
Darius, leader of the Median line;
 While fair Euphrates' ftream our walls protects,
And great Belfhazzar's felf our fate directs.
 War and famine threat in vain,
 While this demi-god fhall reign!
Let Perfia's proftrate king confefs his pow'r,
And Media's monarch dread his vengeful hour.
 On Dura's * ample plain behold
Immortal Belus †, whom the nations own;
 Sublime he ftands in burnifh'd gold,
And richeft offerings his bright altars crown.
To-night his deity we here adore,
And due libations fpeak his mighty pow'r.
 Yet Belus' felf not more we own,
Than great Belfhazzar on Chaldea's throne.
 Great Belfhazzar, like a god,
 Rules the nations with a nod!

To

---

* *Daniel, chap.* iii.

† *See a very fine defcription of the Temple of this Idol.*
  ——— *The tow'ring fane*
Of Bel, Chaldean Jove, furpaffing far
That Doric Temple, which the Elean chiefs
Rais'd to their thunderer from the fpoils of war;
Or that Ionic, where th' Ephefian bow'd
To Dian, queen of heaven. Eight towers arife,
Each above each, immeafurable height,
A monument at once of Eaftern pride,
And flavifh fuperftition, &c. &c.
JUDAH RESTORED, Book I.

To great Belfhazzar be the goblet crown'd!
Belfhazzar's name the echoing roofs rebound!

BELSHAZZAR.

Enough! the kindling rapture fires my brain,
And my heart dances to the flatt'ring founds.
I feel myfelf a god! Why not a god?
What were the deities our fathers worfhipp'd?
What was great Nimrod, our imperial founder?
What, greater Belus, to whofe pow'r divine,
We raife to-night the banquet and the fong;
But youthful heroes, mortal, like myfelf,
Who by their daring earn'd divinity?
They were but men: nay, fome were lefs than men,
Tho' now rever'd as Gods. What was Anubis,
Whom Egypt's fapient fons adore? A dog!
And fhall not I, young, valiant, and a king,
Dare more? do more? be greater than the reft?
I will indulge the thought.——Fill me more wine,
To cherifh and exalt the young idea!   [*He drinks.*
Ne'er did Olympian Jupiter himfelf
Quaff fuch immortal draughts.

Firft COURTIER.

            What cou'd that Canaan,
That heaven in hope, that nothing in poffeffion,
That air-built blifs of the deluded Jews,
That promifs'd land of milk, and flowing honey;
What cou'd that fancied Paradife beftow
To match thefe generous juices?

BELSHAZZAR.

            Hold——enough!
Thou haft rous'd a thought; by Heav'n I will enjoy it;
                  A glo-

A glorious thought ! which will exalt to rapture
The pleasures of the banquet, and bestow
A yet untasted relish of delight.

First COURTIER.
What means the king ?

BELSHAZZAR.
The Jews! saidst thou the Jews?

First COURTIER.
I spoke of that undone, that outcast people,
The tributary creatures of thy pow'r,
The captives of thy will, whose very breath
Hangs on the sov'reign pleasure of the king.

BELSHAZZAR.
When that abandon'd race was hither brought,
Were not the choicest treasures of their temple,
(Devoted to their God, and held most precious)
Among the spoils which grac'd * Nebassar's triumph,
And lodg'd in Babylon?

First COURTIER.
O king! they were.

Second COURTIER.
The Jews, with superstitious awe, behold
These sacred symbols of their ancient faith :
                                        No:

---

* *The name of Nebuchadnezzar not being reducible to
verse, I have adopted that of Nebassar, on the authority of
the ingenious and learned Author of* Judah Restored.

Nor has captivity abated ought
The rev'rend love they bear thefe holy reliques.
'Tho' we deride their law, and fcorn their perfons,
Yet never have we yet to human ufe
Devoted thefe rich veffels, fet apart
To facred purpofes.

B E L S H A Z Z A R.
                    I joy to hear it!
Go—fetch them hither.. They fhall grace our banquet:
Does no one ftir? Belfhazzar difobey'd?
And yet you live! Whence comes this ftrange reluctance?
This new-born rev'rence for the helplefs Jews?
This fear to injure thofe, who can't revenge it?
Send to the facred treafury in hafte,
Let all be hither brought;——who anfwers, dies.
                              [They go out.

The mantling wine a higher joy will yield,
Pour'd from the precious flaggons which adorn'd
Their far-fam'd temple, now in afhes laid.
Oh! 'twill exalt the pleafure in to tranfport,
To gall thofe whining, praying Ifraelites!
I laugh to think what wild difmay will feize them,
When they fhall learn the ufe that has been made
Of all their holy trumpery!
                              [The veffels are brought in.

Second C O U R T I E R.
                              It comes!
A goodly fhew! how bright with gold and gems!
Far fitter for a youthful monarch's board,
Than the cold fhrine of an unheeding God.

                                        B E L-

BELSHAZZAR.

Fill me that maſſy goblet to the brim.
Now, Abraham! let thy wretched race expect
The fable of their faith to be fulfill'd;
Their ſecond temple, and their promis'd king!
Now will they ſee, he's impotent to ſave;
For had he pow'r to help, he would have hinder'd
This profanation.

[*As the king is going to drink, thunder is heard; he ſtarts
from the throne, ſpies a hand, which writes on the
wall theſe words; MENE, MENE, TEKEL, UPHAR-
SIN. He lets fall the goblet, and ſtands in an attitude
of ſpeechleſs horror. All ſtart, and are terrified.*]

Firſt COURTIER, *after a long pauſe.*
Oh, tranſcendent horror!

Second COURTIER.
What may this mean! The king is greatly mov'd!

Third COURTIER.
Nor is it ſtrange—who unappall'd can view it?
Thoſe ſacred cups! I doubt we've gone too far.

Firſt COURTIER.
Obſerve the fear-ſtruck king! his ſtarting eyes
Roll horribly. Thrice he eſſay'd to ſpeak,
And thrice his tongue refus'd.

BELSHAZZAR, *in a low trembling voice.*
Ye myſtic words!
Thou ſemblance of an hand! illuſive forms!

Ye

Ye dire fantaftic images, what are ye ?
Dread fhadows, fpeak ! Explain your horrible meaning!
Ye will not anfwer me.—Yes, yes, I feel
I am a mortal now—My failing limbs
Refufe to bear me up.   I am no god !
Gods do not tremble thus.—Support me; hold me;
Thefe loofen'd joints, thefe knees which fmite each other,
Betray I'm but a man—a weak one too !

Firft COURTIER.

In truth, 'tis paffing ftrange, and full of horror!

BELSHAZZAR.

Send for the learn'd magicians, every fage
Who deal in wizard fpells and magic charms.

                              [*Some go out.*

Firft COURTIER.

How fares my lord the king ?

BELSHAZZAR.

                    Am I a king ?
What pow'r have I ? Ye lying flaves, I am not.
Oh, foul-diftracting fight ! but is it real ?
Perhaps 'tis fancy all, or the wild dream
Of mad diftemperature, the fumes of wine !
I'll look upon't no more !—So—now I'm well !
I am a king again, and know not fear.
And yet my eyes will feek that fatal fpot;
And fondly dwell upon the fight, that blafts them !
Again, 'tis there ! it is not fancy's work.
I fee it ftill ! 'tis written on the wall.
I fee the writing, but the viewlefs writer,
Who, what is he ? Oh, horror ! horror ! horror !

                                                  It

It cannot be the GOD of thefe poor Jews;
For what is He, that he can thus afflict?

Second COURTIER.
Let not my lord the king be thus difmay'd.

Third COURTIER.
Let not a phantom, an illufive fhade,
Difturb the peace of him, who rules the world.

BELSHAZZAR.
No more, ye wretched fycophants ! no more !
The fweeteft note which flatt'ry now can ftrike,
Harfh and difcordant grates upon my foul.
Talk not of power to one fo full of fear,
So weak, fo impotent ? Look on that wall ;
If thou wou'dft footh my foul, explain the writing ;
And thou fhalt be my oracle, my God !
Tell me from whence it came, and what it means,
And I'll believe I am again a king !
Friends ! princes ! eafe my troubled breaft ; and fay,
What do the myftic characters portend ?

Firft COURTIER.
'Tis not in us, O king ! to eafe thy fpirit ;
We are not fkill'd in thofe myfterious arts,
Which wait the midnight ftudies of the fage :
But of the deep diviners thou fhalt learn,
The wife aftrologers, the fage magicians ;
Who, of events unborn, take fecret note,
And hold deep commerce with the unfeen world.

.P   *Enter*

Enter ASTROLOGERS, MAGICIANS,
&c. &c.

BELSHAZZAR.

Approach, ye fages, 'tis the king commands !

[*They kneel.*

ASTROLOGERS.

Hail, mighty king of Babylon !

BELSHAZZAR.

Nay, rife :

I do not need your homage, but your help ;
The world may worfhip, you must counfel me.
He, who declares the fecret of the king,
No common honours fhall await his fkill ;
Our empire fhall be tax'd for his reward,
And he himfelf fhall name the gift he wifhes.
A fplendid fcarlet robe fhall grace his limbs,
His neck a princely chain of gold adorn,
Meet honours for fuch wifdom ; He fhall rule
The third in rank throughout our Babylon.

[*Second* ASTROLOGER.

Such recompence becomes Belfhazzar's bounty.
Let the king fpeak the fecret of his foul ;
Which heard, his humble creatures fhall unfold.

BELSHAZZAR, *points to the wall.*

Be't fo—Look there—behold thofe characters !
Nay, do not ftart, for I will know their meaning !
Ha ! anfwer; fpeak, or inftant death awaits you !
What, dumb ! all dumb ! where is your boafted fkill ;

[*They confer together.*

Keep

Keep them afunder—No confed'racy——
No fecret plots to make your tales agree.
Speak, flaves, and dare to let me know the worft!

Firft ASTROLOGER.

[*They kneel.*

O, let the king forgive his faithful fervants !

Second ASTROLOGER.

O mitigate our threaten'd doom of death ;
If we declare, with mingled grief and fhame,
We cannot tell the fecret of the king,
Nor what thefe myftic characters portend !

BELSHAZZAR.

Off with their heads ! Ye fhall not live an hour !
Curfe on your fhallow arts, your lying fcience !
'Tis thus you practife on the credulous world,
Who think you wife, becaufe themfelves are weak !
But, mifcreants, ye fhall die ! the pow'r to punifh
Is all that I have left me of a king.

Firft COURTIER.

Great Sir ! fufpend their punifhment awhile.
Behold fage Nitocris, thy royal mother !

BELSHAZZAR.

My mother here !

Enter QUEEN.

QUEEN.

O my mifguided fon !
Well may'ft thou wonder to behold me here :

For

For I have ever fhunn'd this fcene of riot,
Where wild Intemperance and difhonour'd Mirth
Hold feftival impure. Yet, O Belfhazzar!
I cou'd not hear the wonders which befel,
And leave thee to the workings of defpair:
For, fpite of all the anguifh of my foul
At thy offences, I'm thy mother ftill!
Againft the folemn purpofe I had forin'd
Never to mix in this unhallow'd crowd,
The wond'rous ftory of the myftic writing,
Of ftrange and awful import, brings me here;.
If haply I may fhew fome likely means
To fathom this dark myftery.

BELSHAZZAR.

                    Speak, C queen!
My liftn'ning foul fhall hang upon thy words,
And prompt obedience follow them!

QUEEN.

                    Then hear me
Among the captive tribes, which hither came
To grace Nebaffar's triumph, there was brought
A youth nam'd Daniel, favour'd by high Heav'n.
With pow'r to look into the fecret page
Of dim futurity's myfterious volume.
The fpirit of the holy Gods is in him;
No vifion fo obfcure, no fate fo dark,
No fentence fo perplex'd, but he can folve it:
Can trace each crooked labyrinth of thought,
Each winding maze of doubt, and make it clear,
And palpable to fenfe. He twice explain'd
The monarch's myftic dreams. The holy feer

                                        Saw,

Saw, with prophetic spirit, what befel
The king long after.   For his wond'rous skill
He was rewarded, honour'd, and caress'd,
And with the rulers of Chaldea rank'd :
Tho' now, alas! thrown by ; his services
Forgotten or neglected ; such the meed
Which virtue finds in courts.

BELSHAZZAR.
                              Dispatch with speed
A message, to command the holy man
To meet us on the instant.

NITOCRIS.
                              I already
Have sent to ask his presence at the palace ;
And, lo! he comes.

Enter DANIEL.

BELSHAZZAR.
   Welcome, thrice venerable sage! approach.
Art thou that Daniel, whom my great forefather
Brought hither with the captive tribes of Judah?

DANIEL.
   I am that Daniel.

BELSHAZZAR.
                              Pardon, holy Prophet ;
Nor let a just resentment of thy wrongs,
And long neglected merit, shut thy heart
Against a king's request, a suppliant king !
                                        DANIEL.

DANIEL.

The GOD I worſhip teaches to forgive.

BELSHAZZAR.

Then l● thy words bring comfort to my ſoul.
I've heard the ſpirit of the Gods is in thee;
That thou can'ſt look into the fates of men,
With preſcience more than human!

DANIEL.

     Hold, O king!
Wiſdom is from above, 'tis GOD's own gift.
I of myſelf am nothing; but from Him
· The little knowledge I poſſeſs, I hold:
To him be all the glory!

BELSHAZZAR.

     Then, O Daniel!
If thou indeed doſt boaſt that wond'rous gift,
That faculty divine; look there, and tell me!
O ſay, what mean thoſe myſtic characters?
Remove this load of terror from my ſoul;
And honours, ſuch as kings can give, await thee:
Thou ſhalt be great beyond thy ſoul's ambition,
And rich above thy wildeſt dream of wealth:
Clad in the ſcarlet robe our nobles wear,
And grac'd with princely enſigns, thou ſhalt ſtand
Near our own throne, and third within our empire.

DANIEL.

O mighty king! thy gifts with thee remain,
And let thy high rewards on others fall.
The princely enſign, nor the ſcarlet robe,

            Nor

Nor yet to be the third within thy realm,
Can touch the foul of Daniel. Honour, fame,
All that the world calls great, thy crown itſelf,
Cou'd never ſatisfy the vaſt ambition
Of an immortal ſpirit, which aſpires
To an eternal crown, a crown of glory!

Firſt COURTIER. [Aſide.

Our prieſts teach no ſuch notions.

DANIEL.

Yet, O king!
Tho' all unmov'd by grandeur, or by gift,
I will unfold the high decrees of Heav'n,
And ſtrait declare the myſtery.

BELSHAZZAR.

Speak, O Prophet!

DANIEL.

Prepare to hear, what kings have ſeldom heard;
Prepare to hear, what theſe have never told thee:
Prepare to hear the TRUTH. The mighty GOD,
Who rules the ſceptres and the hearts of kings,
Gave thy renown'd * forefather here to reign,
With ſuch extent of empire, weight of pow'r,
And greatneſs of dominion, the wide earth
Trembled beneath the terror of his name,
And kingdoms ſtood or fell as he decreed.
Oh! dangerous pinnacle of pow'r ſupreme!
Who can ſtand ſafe upon its treach'rous top,

Behold

---

* *Nebuchadnezzar.*

Behold the gazing proftrate world below,
Whom dcp'h and diftance into pigmies fhrink,
And not grow giddy? Babylon's great king
Forgot he was a man, a helplefs man,
Subject to pain, and fin, and dea'h, like others!
But who fhall fight againft Omnipotence?
Or who hath harden'd his obdurate heart
Againft the Majefty of Heav'n, and profper'd?
The GOD he had infulted was aveng'd;
From empire, from the joys of focial life,
He drove him forth; extinguifh'd reafon's lamp,
Quench'd that bright fpark of deity within;
Compell'd him, with the foreft brutes, to roam
For fcanty pafture; and the mountain dews
Fell, cold and wet, on his defencelefs head:
Till he confefs'd—Let men, let monarchs hear!—
Till he confefs'd, PRIDE WAS NOT MADE FOR MAN!

NITOCRIS.

O, awful inftance of divine difpleafure!

BELSHAZZAR.

Proceed! My foul is wrapt in fix'd attention!

DANIEL.

O king! thy grandfire not in vain had finn'd;
If, from his error, thou had'ft learnt the truth.
The ftory of his fall thou oft haft heard,
But has it taught thee wifdom? Thou, like him,
Haft been elate with pow'r, and mad with pride.
Like him, thou haft defy'd the Living GOD.
Nay, to bold thoughts, haft added deeds more bold.
Thou haft out-wrought the pattern he bequeath'd thee,

And

And quite outgone example; haft prophan'd,
With impious hand, the veffels of the Temple :
Thofe veffels, fanctified to holieft ufe,
Thou haft polluted with unhallow'd lips,
And made the inftruments of foul debauch.
Thou haft ador'd the gods of wood and ftone,
Vile, fenfelefs deities, the work of hands ;
But HE, THE KING OF KINGS, AND LORD OF LORDS,
In whom exifts thy life, thy foul, thy breath,
On whom thy being hangs, thou haft deny'd.

Firft COURTIER.

[A fide to the others.

With what an holy boldnefs he reproves him!

Second COURTIER.

Such is the fearlefs confidence of virtue!
And fuch the righteous courage thofe maintain,
Who plead the caufe of truth! The fmalleft word,
He utters, had been death to half the court.

BELSHAZZAR.

Now let the myftic writing be explain'd,
Thrice venerable fage!

DANIEL.

O mighty king!
Hear then its awful import: *God has number'd*
Thy days of royalty, and foon will end them.
The All-wife has weigh'd thee in the even balance
Of his own holy law, and finds thee wanting:
And laft, Thy kingdom fhall be wrefted from thee;
And know, the Mede and Perfian fhall poffefs it.

Q.   BEL.

B E L S H A Z Z A R.

[He starts up.

Prophet, when shall this be?

D A N I E L.

In God's own time:
Here my commission ends; I may not utter
More than thou hast heard; but O! remember, king!
Thy days are number'd; here, repent, and live!

B E L S H A Z Z A R.

Say, Prophet, what can penitence avail?
If Heav'n's decrees immutably are fix'd,
Can pray'rs avert our fate?

D A N I E L.

They change our hearts,
And thus dispose Omnipotence to mercy.
'Tis man that alters, God is still the same.
Conditional are all Heav'n's covenants:
And when th' uplifted thunder is with-held,
'Tis pray'r that deprecates th' impending bolt.
Good * Hezekiah's days were number'd too;
But penitence and tears were mighty pleas;
At Mercy's throne they never plead in vain.

[He is going.

B E L S H A Z Z A R.

Stay, Prophet, and receive thy promis'd gift:
The scarlet robe, and princely chain, are thine:

And

---

* 2 *Chron. chap.* xxxiii. *Also Isaiah, chap.* xxxviii.

And let my heralds publifh through the land,
That Daniel ftands, in dignity and pow'r,
The third in Babylon.   Thefe juft rewards
Thou well may'ft claim, though fad thy prophecy!

QUEEN.

Be not deceiv'd, my fon! nor let thy foul
Snatch an uncertain moment's treach'rous reft,
On the dread brink of that tremendous gulf
Which yawns beneath thee.

DANIEL.

                    O unhappy king!
Know what *muft* happen once, *may* happen foon.
Remember, that 'tis terrible to meet
Great evils unprepar'd! and, O Belfhazzar!
In the wild moment of difmay and death,
Remember thou waft warn'd! and, O! remember,
Warnings defpis'd are condemnations then!
                    [*Exeunt Daniel and Queen.*

BELSHAZZAR.

'Tis well—my foul fhakes off its load of care:
'Tis only the obfcure is terrible.
Imagination frames events unknown,
In wild fantaftic fhapes of hideous ruin;
And what it fears, creates!—I know the worft;
And awful is that worft, as fear could feign:
But diftant are the ills, I have to dread!
What is remote may be uncertain too!
Ha! Princes! hope breaks in!—This may not be!

Q 2   *Firft*

First COURTIER.

Perhaps this Daniel is in league with Perfia ;
And brib'd by Cyrus to report thefe horrors,
To weaken and impede the mighty plans
Of thy imperial mind !

BELSHAZZAR.
'Tis very like.

Second COURTIER.

Return we to the banquet.

BELSHAZZAR.
Dare we venture ?

Third COURTIER.

Let not this dreaming Seer difturb the king.
Againft the pow'r of Cyrus, and the Mede,
Is Babylon fecure. Her brazen gates
Mock all attempts to force them. Proud Euphrates, .
A watry bulwark, guards our ample city
From all affailants. And within the walls
Of this ftupendous capital are lodg'd
Such vaft provifions, fuch exhauftlefs ftores, .
As a twice ten years fiege could never wafte !

BELSHAZZAR.
Embraces him.
My better genius ! To the banquet then !

[*As they are going to refume their places at the banquet,
a dreadful uproar is heard, tumultuous cries, and war-
like founds. All ftand terrified. Enter foldiers, with
their fwords drawn, and wounded.*

SOLDIER.

SOLDIER.

Oh, helpleſs Babylon! Oh, wretched king!
Chaldea is no more, the Mede has conquer'd!
The victor Cyrus, like a mighty torrent,
Comes ruſhing on, and marks his way with ruin!

BELSHAZZAR.

Impoſſible! Villain and ſlave thou ly'ſt!
Euphrates and the brazen gates ſecure us.
While thoſe remain, Belſhazzar laughs at danger.

SOLDIER.

Euphrates is diverted from its courſe,
The brazen gates are burſt, the city's taken,
Thyſelf a priſ'ner, and thy empire loſt.

BELSHAZZAR.

Oh, Prophet! I remember thee too ſoon!
[*He runs out. They follow, in the utmoſt confuſion.*

Enter ſeveral JEWS, MEDES, *and* BABY-
LONIANS.

Firſt JEW.

He comes, he comes! the long predicted prince,
Cyrus! the deſtin'd inſtrument of Heav'n,
To free our captive nation, and reſtore
JEHOVAH's Temple! Carnage marks his way,
And conqueſt ſits upon his plume-crown'd helm;

Second JEW.

What noiſe is that?

Firſt J E W.
        Hark! 'Tis Belſhazzar's voice!'

B E L S H A Z Z A R.   [*Without.*

O Soldier! ſpare my life, and aid my flight;
Such treaſures ſhall reward the gentle deed,
As Perſia never ſaw! I'll be thy ſlave;
I'll yield my crówn to Cyrus, I'll adore
His Gods and thine—I'll kneel and kiſs thy feet,
And worſhip thee—It is not much I aſk—
I'll live in bondage, beggary, and pain,
So thou but let me live!

S O L D I E R.
        Die, tyrant die!

B E L S H A Z Z A R.
O Daniel! Daniel! Daniel!

Enter S O L D I E R.

S O L D I E R.
        Belſhazzar's dead!
The wretched king breath'd out his furious ſoul
In that tremendous groan.

Firſt J E W.
        Belſhazzar's dead!
Then, Judah! art thou free! The tyrant's fall'n!
Jeruſalem, Jeruſalem is free!

B E L-

BELSHAZZAR.

PART III.

Enter DANIEL *and* JEWS.

DANIEL.

BEL boweth down *, and haughty Nebo ftoops!
The idols fall ; the God and worſhipper
Together fall ! together they bow down !
Each other, or themſelves, they cannot ſave.
O, Babylon! where is thy refuge now ?
Thy wiſdom and thy knowledge, meant to ſave,
Pervert thee ; and thy bleſſing is thy bane !
Where are thy brutiſh deities, Chaldea ?
Where are thy gods of gold ?—Oh, Lord of life !
Thou very GOD! ſo fall thy foes before thee!

Firſt JEW.

So fell beneath the terrors of thy name
The idol Chemoſh, Moab's empty truſt;

So

---

* *Iſaiah, chap.* xlvi.

So Ammonitiſh Moloch ſunk before thee;
So fell Philiſtine Dagon: ſo ſhall fall,
To time's remoteſt period, all thy foes!

DANIEL.

Not for myſelf, O Judah! but for thee,
I ſhed theſe tears of joy. For I no more
Muſt view the cedars which adorn the brow
Of Syrian Lebanon; no more ſhall ſee
Thy pleaſant ſtream, O Jordan! nor the flocks,
Which whiten all the mountains of Judea;
Nor Carmel's heights, nor Sharon's flow'ry vales.
I muſt remain in Babylon! So Heav'n,
To whoſe awards I bow me, has decreed.
I ne'er ſhall ſee thee, Salem! I am old;
And few, and toilſome, are my days to come.
But we ſhall meet in thoſe celeſtial climes,
Compar'd with which created glories ſink:
Where ſinners ſhall have pow'r to harm no more,
And martyr'd Virtue reſts her weary head.
Tho' ere my day of promis'd grace ſhall come,
I ſhall be try'd by perils ſtrange and new;
Nor ſhall I taſte of death, ſo have I learn'd,
'Till I have ſeen the captive tribes reſtor'd.

First J E W.

And ſhall we view, once more, thy hallow'd tow'rs,
Imperial Salem?

DANIEL.

Yes, my youthful friends!
You ſhall behold the ſecond * temple riſe,

With

---

* Ezra, chap. i.

With grateful ecftacy : but we, your fires,
Now bent with hoary age ; we, whofe charm'd eyes
Beheld the matchlefs glories of the firft,
Shou'd weep, rememb'ring what we once had feen,
That model of perfection!

Second JEW.
Never more
Shall fuch another ftructure grace the earth ?

DANIEL.
Well have you borne affliction, men of Judah!
Well have fuftain'd your portion of diftrefs ;
And unrepining, drank the bitter dregs
Of adverfe fortune! Happier days await you.
O guard againft the perils of fuccefs !
Profperity diffolves the yielding foul,
And the bright Sun of fhining fortune melts
The firmeft virtue down.   Beware, my friends,
Be greatly cautious of profperity!
Defend your fliding hearts ; and, trembling, think
How thofe, who buffeted affliction's waves
With vig'rous virtue, funk in Pleafure's calm.
He *, who of fpecial grace had been allow'd
To rear the hallow'd fane to Ifrael's God,
By wealth corrupted, and by eafe debauch'd,
Forfook the God to whom he rais'd the fane ;
And, funk in fenfual floth, confum'd his days,
In vile idolatrous rites!——Nor think, my fons,
That virtue in fequefter'd *folitude*
R   Is

---

* *Solomon.*

Is always found. Within the inmoft foul
The hidden tempter lurks ; nor lefs betrays,
In the ftill, feeming fafety of retreat,
Than where the treach'rous world delufive fmiles.
Who thinks himfelf fecure, is half undone ;
For fin, unwatch'd, may reach the fanctuary :
No place preferves us from it. Righteous Lot
Stemm'd the ftrong current of corruption's tide,
Ev'n in polluted Sodom ; fafe he liv'd,
While circumfpective Virtue's watchful eye
Was anxioufly awake : but in the fhade,
Far from the threat'ning perils which alarm
With vifible temptation, fecret fin
Enfnar'd him ; in fecurity he fell.

Second JEW.

Thy prudent counfels in our hearts fhall live,
As if a pen of adamant had grav'd them.

Firft JEW.

The dawn approaches ; let us part, my friend,
Secure of peace, fince tyranny is fall'n !

DANIEL.

So perifh all thine enemies, O LORD !
So mighty GOD ! fhall perifh all, who feek
Corrupted pleafures in the turbid waves
Of life's polluted ftream ; and madly quit
The living fountain of perennial grace !

THE END.

PERSONS of the DRAMA.

DARIUS, King of MEDIA and BABYLON.

PHARNACES,
SORANUS, } Courtiers, enemies to Daniel.

ARASPES, a young MEDIAN Lord, friend and convert of DANIEL.

DANIEL.

SCENE, The City of BABYLON.

☞ The Subject of this drama is taken from the Sixth Chapter of the Book of the Prophet DANIEL.

R 2

DANIEL:

A

SACRED DRAMA.

PART I.

The Righteous is delivered out of trouble, and the Wicked
cometh in his ſtead.——PROVERBS of SOLOMON.

On peut des plus grands rois ſurprendre la juſtice.
Incapable de tromper,
Ils ont peine a s'echapper
Des pieges de l'artifice.
Un cœur noble ne peut ſoupçonner en autrui.
La baſſeſſe et la malice
Qu'il ne ſent point en lui.

ESTHER. TRAGÉDIE de RACINE.

PHARNACES, SORANUS.

PHARNACES.

YES!—I have noted, with a jealous eye,
The pow'r of this new fav'rite! Daniel reigns,
And not Darius! Daniel guides the ſprings
Which move this mighty empire! High he ſits,
Supreme in favour both with prince and people!

Where

Where is the fpirit of our Median lords,
Tamely to crouch and bend the fupple knee
To this new god? By Mithras, 'tis too much!
Shall great Arbaces' race to Daniel bow?
A foreigner, a captive, and a Jew?
Something muft be devis'd, and that right foon,
To fhake his credit.

SORANUS.

            Rather hope to fhake ·
The mountain pine, whofe twifting fibres clafp
The earth, deep rooted! Rather hope to fhake ·
The Scythian Taurus from his central bafe!
No—Daniel fits too abfolute in pow'r,
Too firm in favour, for the keeneft fhaft
Of nicely-aiming jealoufy to reach him. ·

PHARNACES.

  Rather he fits too high to fit fecurely.
Haft thou then liv'd in courts? haft thou grown grey,
Beneath the mafk a fubtil ftatefman wears
To hide his fecret foul, and doft not know
That, of all fickle Fortune's tranfient gifts,
Favour is moft deceitful? 'Tis a beam,
Which darts uncertain brightnefs for a moment!
The faint, precarious, fickly fhine of pow'r;
Giv'n without merit, by caprice withdrawn.
No trifle is fo fmall as what obtains,
Save that which lofes it. It is a breath,
Which hangs upon a fmile! A look, a word,
A frown, the air-built tow'r of favour fhakes,
And down the unfubftantial fabric falls!
Darius, juft and clement as he is,

If

If I miſtake not, may be wrought upon
By prudent wiles, by Flattery's pleaſant cup,
Adminiſter'd with caution.

SORANUS.

                But the means?
For Daniel's life (a foe muſt grant him that)
Is ſo replete with goodneſs, ſo adorn'd
With every virtue, ſo exactly ſquar'd
By wiſdom's niceſt rules, that 'twere moſt hard
To charge him with the ſhadow of offence.
Pure is his fame, as Scythia's mountain ſnows,
When not a breath pollutes them! O Pharnaces!
I've ſcann'd the action's of his daily life
With all th' induſtrious malice of a foe ;
And nothing meets mine eye but deeds of honour!
In office pure ; for equitable acts
Renown'd : in juſtice and impartial truth,
The Grecian Themis is not more ſevere.

PHARNACES.

   By yon bright ſun, thou blazon'ſt forth his praiſe,
As if with rapture thou didſt read the page,
Where theſe fair deeds are written!

SORANUS.

               Thou miſtak'ſt.
I only meant to ſhew, what cauſe we have
To hate and fear him. I but meant to paint
His popular virtues, and his dang'rous merit.
Then for devotion, and religious zeal,
Who ſo renown'd as Daniel? Of his law
Obſervant in th' extreme. Thrice ev'ry day,

                         With

With proftrate rev'rence, he adores his God:
With fuperftitious awe his face he turns
Tow'rds his belov'd Jerufalem; as if
Some local, partial God might there be found
To hear his fupplication.   No affair
Of ftate; no bufinefs fo importunate;
No pleafure fo alluring; no employ
Of fuch high import, to feduce his zeal
From this obfervance due!

PHARNACES.

There, there he falls!
Enough, my friend! His piety deftroys him.
There, at the very footftool of his God,
Where he implores protection, there I'll crufh him!

SORANUS.

What means Pharnaces?

PHARNACES.

Afk not what I mean!
The new idea floating in my brain,
Has yet receiv'd no form. 'Tis yet too foon
To give it body, circumftance, or breath.
The feeds of mighty deeds are lab'ring here,
And ftruggling for a birth! 'Tis near the hour
The king is wont to fummon us to council.
Ere that, this big conception of my mind
I'll fhape to form and being.   Thou, meanwhile,
Convene our chofen friends; for I fhall need
The aid of all your counfels, and the weight
Of grave authority.

SORANUS.

Who fhall be trufted?

PHAR-

PHARNACES.

With our immediate motive, none, except
A chofen band of friends, who moft repine
At Daniel's Exaltation.   But the fcheme
I meditate, muft be difclos'd to all
Who bear high office; all our Median rulers,
Princes and captains, prefidents and lords;
. All muft affemble! 'Tis a common caufe;
All but the young Arafpes, he inclines
T. Daniel and his God.   He fits attent,
With ravifh'd ears, to liften to his lore:
With rev'rence names Jerufalem, and reads
The volume of the law! No more he bows,
To hail the golden Ruler of the Day;
But looks for fome great Prophet, greater far,
So they pretend, than Mithras! From him, therefore,
Conceal whate'er of injury is devis'd
'Gainft Daniel.   Be it too thy care to-day,
To keep him from the council.

SORANUS.

                     'Tis well thought.
'Tis now about the hour of Daniel's pray'r,
Arafpes too is with him; and to-day
They will not fit in council. Hafte we then!
Defigns of high importance, once conceiv'd,
Shou'd be accomplifh'd.   Genius to difcern,
And courage to atchieve, defpife the aid
Of ling'ring circumfpection.   The keen fpirit
Seizes the prompt occafion, and at once
, Plans and performs, refolves and executes!

                                       DANIEL.

DANIEL.

PART II.

SCENE, Daniel's Houſe.

DANIEL, ARASPES.

ARASPES.

PROCEED, proceed, thrice venerable ſage!
Enlighten my dark mind with this new ray,
This dawning of ſalvation! Tell me more
Of this expected King! this Prince of Peace!
This Promiſe of the nations! this great Hope
Of anxious Iſraël! This mighty Prophet!
This Balm of Gilead, which ſhall heal the wounds
Of univerſal nature! this MESSIAH!
Redeemer, ſaviour, ſufferer, victim, GOD!

DANIEL.

Enough to animate our faith, we know,
But not enough to ſoothe the curious pride
Of vain philoſophy! Were all reveal'd,

S

Hope

Hope wou'd have then no object, GOD no fear,
And faith no exercife! Enough to cheer
Our path we fee, the reft is hid in clouds;
And Heav'n's own fhadows reft upon the view!

A R A S P E S.

Go on, bleft fage! I cou'd for ever hear,
Untir'd, thy admonition! Tell me, how
I fhall obtain the favour of that GOD
I but begin to know.

D A N I E L.

                              By holy deeds,
By deep humility, by faith unfeign'd.
O Faith *, thou wonder-working principle!
Eternal fubftance of our prefent hope,
Thou evidence of things invifible!
What cannot man fuftain, fuftain'd by thee?
The time wou'd fail, and the bright ftar of day
Wou'd quench his beams in ocean, and refign
His empire to the filver queen of night;
And fhe again defcend the fteep of heav'n,
If I fhou'd tell what wonders Faith atchiev'd,
By Gideon, Barak, and the fapient feer,
Elkanah's fon; the pious Gileadite,
Ill-fated Jephthah! He of † Zorah too,
In ftrength unequall'd; and the fhepherd-king,
Who flew the giant of Gath! Why fhou'd I tell
Of holy Prophets, who, by conquering Faith,
Wrought deeds incredible to mortal fenfe;

                              Vanquifh'd

---

* *Hebrews, chap.* xi.   † *Samfon.*

Vanquish'd contending kingdoms, quell'd the rage
Of furious pestilence, extinguish'd fire?
Victorious Faith! others by thee endur'd
Exile, difgrace, captivity, and death!
Some, uncomplaining, bore (nor be it deem'd
The meaneft exercife of well-try'd Faith)
The bitter taunts of undeferv'd reproach;
Defpifing fhame, that death to human pride!

ARASPES.
How fhall this faith be fought?

DANIEL.
     By earnéft pray'r.
Solicit firft the wifdom from above;
Wifdom *, whofe fruits are purity and peace!
Wifdom! that bright intelligence, which fat
Supreme, when with his golden † compaffes
Th' Eternal plann'd the fabric of the world,
Produc'd his fair idea into light,
And faid, That all was good! Wifdom, bleft beam!'
The brightnefs of the everlafting light!
The fpotlefs mirror of the pow'r of GOD!
The reflex image of th' all-perfect mind!
A ftream tranflucent, flowing from the fource
Of glory infinite; a cloudlefs light!
Defilement cannot touch, nor fin pollute
Her unftain'd purity! Not Ophir's gold,

S 2

Nor

---

* *Wifdom of Solomon, chap.* vii.

† *See Paradife Loft, book* vii. *l.* 225; *alfo Proverbs, chap.* viii. *ver.* 27.

Nor Ethiopia's gems can match her price!
The diamond of the mine is pale before her!
And, like the oil Elisha's bounty bless'd,
She is a treafure which doth grow by ufe,.
And multiply by fpending! fhe contains,
Within herfelf, the fum of excellence,
If riches are defir'd, wifdom is wealth!.
If prudence, where fhall keen invention find?
Artificer more cunning? If renown,
In her right-hand it comes! If piety,
Are not her labours virtues? If the lore
Which fage experience teaches, lo! fhe fcans
Antiquity's dark truths; the paft fhe knows,
Anticipates the future; not by arts
Forbidden, of Chaldean forcerer;
But from the piercing ken of deep foreknowledge;
From her fure fcience of the human heart;
Weighing effects with caufes, ends with means;
And from the probable the certain forms,
With palpable conjecture!

ARASPES.

                    Now, O Prophet!
Explain the fecret doubts which rack my mind,
And my weak fenfe confound.   Give me fome line
To found the depths of Providence! O fay,
Why the ungodly profper? why their root
Shoots deep, and their thick branches flourifh fair,
Like the green bay tree? why the righteous man,
Like tender plants, to fhiv'ring winds expos'd,
Is ftripp'd and torn, in naked virtue bare,
And nipp'd by cruel forrow's biting blaft?
Explain, O Daniel! thefe myfterious ways,

To my faint apprehenſion! For as yet
I've much to learn.. Fair Truth's immortal ſun
Is ſometimes hid in clouds; not that her light
Is in itſelf defective; but obſcur'd
By my weak prejudice, imperfect Faith,
And all the thouſand cauſes which obſtruct
The growth of virtue.

DANIEL.
                    Follow me, Araſpes†
Within, thou ſhalt peruſe the ſacred page,
The book of Life eternal! there thou wilt ſee
The END of the ungodly; thou wilt own
How ſhort their longeſt period; wilt perceive
How black a night ſucceeds their brighteſt day!
Weigh well this book; and may the Spirit of Grace,
Who ſtamp'd the ſeal of truth on the bleſs'd page,
Deſcend into thy ſoul, remove thy doubts,
Clear the perplex'd, and ſolve the intricate,
'Till Faith be loſt in ſight, and Hope in joy!

DANIEL.

DANIEL.

PART III.

DARIUS *on his throne.* PHARNACES, SO-
RANUS, PRINCES, PRESIDENTS,
and COURTIERS.

PHARNACES.

O KING Darius, live for ever!

DARIUS.

              Welcome!
Welcome, my princes, prefidents and friends!
Now tell me, has your wifdom ought devis'd
To ferve the common weal? In our new empire,
Subdued Chaldea, is there ought remains
Your prudence can fuggeft, to ferve the ftate,
To benefit the fubject, to redrefs
And raife the injur'd? to affift th' opprefs'd,
And humble the oppreffor? If you know,

Speak freely, princes! Wherefore am I king,
Except to poife the awful fcale of juftice
With even hand; to minifter to want,
To blefs the nations with a lib'ral rule,
Vicegerent of th' eternal Oroinafdes!

PHARNACES.

So abfolute thy wifdom, mighty king!
All counfel were fuperfluous.

DARIUS.

Hold, Pharnaces.
No flatt'ry, prince; it is the death of virtue;
Who gives it is of all mankind the loweft,
Save he who takes it. Monarchs are but men;
As feeble and as frail as thofe they rule,
And born, like them, to die. The Lydian king,
Unhappy Crœfus! lately fat aloft,
Almoft above mortality now fee him,
Sunk to the vile condition of a flave,
He fwells the train of Cyrus! I, like him,
To mis'ry am obnoxious. See this throne:
This very throne the great * Nebaffar fill'd;
Yet hence his pride expell'd him! Yonder wall,
The dread terrific writing to the eyes
Of proud Belfhazzar fhew'd; fad monuments
Of Heav'n's tremendous vengeance! and fhall I,
Unwarn'd by fuch examples, cherifh pride?
Yet to their dire calamities I owe
The brighteft gem that gliftens in my crown,

Sage

---

* *Nebuchadnezzar.*

Sage Daniel. If my ſpeech have ought of worth,
Or if my life with ought of good be grac'd,
To him'alone I owe it.

SORANUS. [*Aſide to Pharnaces.*

Now, Pharnaces,
Will he run o'er, and dwell upon his praiſe,
As if we ne'er had heard it; nay, will ſwell
The nauſeous catalogue with many a virtue
His own fond fancy coins.

PHARNACES.

O, great Darius!
Let thine unworthy ſervant's words find grace;
And meet acceptance in his royal ear,
Who ſubjugates the Eaſt! Let not the king
With anger hear my pray'r.

DARIUS.

arnaces, ſpeak!
I know thou lov'ſt me: I but meant to chide
Thy flatt'ry, not reprove thee for thy zeal.
Speak boldly, friends, as man ſhou'd ſpeak to man.
Periſh the barb'rous maxims of the Eaſt,
Which baſely wou'd enſlave the free-born mind,
And plunder it of the beſt gift of Heav'n,
Its liberty!

PHARNACES.

Then, O Darius, hear me!
Thy princes, and the captains of thy bands,
Thy preſidents, the governors who rule
Thy provinces, and I, thine humble creature

(Leſs

~(Lefs than the leaft in merit, but in love,
In zeal, and duty, equal with the firft;)
We have devis'd a meafure to confirm
Thy infant empire; to eftablifh here
Thy pow'r with firm dominion, and fecure
Thy growing greatnefs paft the pow'r of change.

DARIUS.

I am prepar'd to hear thee. Speak, Pharnaces!

PHARNACES.

The wretched Babylonians long have groan'd
Beneath the rule of princes, weak or rafh.
The rod of pow'r was falfely fway'd alike,
By feeble Merodach, and fierce Belfhazzar.
One let the flacken'd reins too loofely float
Upon the people's neck, and loft his pow'r
By nervelefs relaxation. He, who follow'd,
Held with a tyrant's hand the cruel curb,
And check'd the groaning nation till it bled.
On diff'rent rocks they met one common ruin.
Their edicts were irrefolute, their laws
Were feebly plann'd, their councils ill-advis'd;
Now fo relax'd, and now fo overftrain'd,
That the tir'd people, wearied with the weight
They long have borne, will foon difdain controul,
Tread on all rule, and fpurn the hand that guides 'em.

DARIUS.

But fay what remedy?

T   PHAR-

PHARNACES.

That too, O king!
Thy fervants have provided. Hitherto
They bear the yoke fubmiffive. But to fix
Thy pow'r, and their obedience ; to reduce
All hearts to thy dominion, yet avoid
Thofe deeds of cruelty thy nature ftarts at—
Thou fhou'd'ft begin by fome imperial act
Of abfolute dominion, yet unftain'd
By ought of barbarous. For know, O king !
Wholefome feverity, if wifely rul'd,
With fober difcipline, procures refpect,
More than the lenient counfels and weak meafures,
Of frail irrefolution.

DARIUS.

Now proceed
To thy requeft.

PHARNACES.

Not I, but all requeft it.
Be thy imperial edict iffued ftrait,
And let a firm decree this day be pafs'd,
Irrevocable, as our Median laws
Ordain, that for the fpace of thirty days,
No fubject in thy realm fhall ought requeft
Of God, or man, except of thee, O king!

DARIUS.

Wherefore this ftrange decree ?

PHARNACES.

'Twill fix the crown
With lafting fafety on thy royal brow ;

And

And by a bloodlefs means preferve th' obedience
Of this new empire. Think how much 'twill raife
Thy high renown ! 'Twill make thy name rever'd,
And popular beyond example. What !
To be as Heav'n, difpenfing good and ill
For thirty days ! With thine own ears to hear
Thy people's wants, with thine own lib'ral hands
To blefs thy fuppliant fubjects ! O Darius !
Thou'lt feem as bounteous as a giving God !
And reign in ev'ry heart in Babylon,
As well as Media. What a glorious ftate,
To be the bleffed arbiter of good ;
The firft efficient caufe of happinefs !
To fcatter mercies with a plenteous hand,
And to be bleft thyfelf in bleffing others !

DARIUS.

Is this the gen'ral wifh ?

> [*The Princes and Courtiers kneel.*

Chief PRESIDENT.

Of one, of all.
Behold thy princes, prefidents, and lords,
Thy counfellors, and captains ! See, O king !

> [*Prefenting the Edict.*

Behold the inftrument our zeal has drawn ;
The edict is prepar'd. We only wait
The confirmation of thy gracious word,
And thy imperial fignet.

DARIUS.

Say, Pharnaces,
What penalty awaits the man who dares
Tranfgrefs our mandate ?

PHAR-

PHARNACES.
               Inftant death, O king !.
This ftatute fays, " Should any fubject dare
" Petition, for the fpace of thirty days,
" Of God, or man, except of thee, O king !
" He fhall be thrown into yon' dreadful den
" Of hungry lions !"

D A R I U S.
             Hold ! Methinks a deed
Of fuch importance fhou'd be wifely weigh'd.

P H A R N A C E S.
We have revolv'd it, mighty king, with care,.
With clofeft fcrutiny.

D A R I U S.
             I'm fatisfy'd.
Then to your wifdom I commit me, princes !
Behold the royal fignet, fee, 'tis done !

P H A R N A C E S.   [*Afide*.
There Daniel fell ! That fignet feal'd his doom!

D A R I U S.   [*After a paufe*.
Let me reflect !—Sure I have been too rafh !
Why fuch intemperate hafte ? But you are wife ;
And would not counfel this fevere decree
But for the wifeft purpofe. Yet, methinks
I might have weigh'd, and in my mind revolv'd
This ftatute, ere, the royal fignet ftamp'd,
It had been paft repeal ! Sage Daniel too !
My counfellor, my venerable friend,

                                             He

He fhou'd have been confulted ; for his wifdom
I ftill have found oracular.

PHARNACES.

Mighty king !
'Tis as it fhould be ! The decree is paft
Irrevocable, as the ftedfaft law
Of Mede and Perfian, which can never change.
Thofe who obferve it live, as is moft meet,
High in thy grace ; who violate it, die.

DANIEL:

PART IV.

SCENE, DANIEL's Houfe.

DANIEL, ARASPES.

ARASPES.

OH, holy Daniel ! prophet, father, friend !
I come, the wretched meſſenger of ill !
Thy foes complot thy death.   For what can mean
This new-made law, extorted from the king,
Almoft by force ? What can it mean, O Daniel !
But to involve thee in the toils they fpread
To fnare thy precious life ?

DANIEL.

DANIEL.

How! was the king,
Confenting to this edict?

ARASPES.

They furpris'd
His eafy nature; took him when his heart
Was foften'd by their blandifhments! They wore
The mafk of public virtue to deceive him.
Beneath the fpecious name of gen'ral good,
They wrought him to their purpofes: no time
Allow'd him to deliberate.   One fhort hour,
Another moment, and his foul had gain'd
Her natural tone of virtue.

DANIEL.

That great Pow'r
Who fuffers evil, only to produce
Some unfeen good, permits that this fhou'd be:
And, HE permitting, I, well pleas'd, refign!
Retire, my friend! This is my fecond hour
Of daily pray'r.   Anon we'll meet again!
Here, in the open face of that bright fun
Thy fathers worfhipp'd, will I offer up,
As is my rule, petition to our GOD,
For thee, for me, for Solyma, for all!

ARASPES.

Oh, ftay! what mean'ft thou! fure thou haft not heard
The edict of the king? I thought, but now,
Thou knew'ft its purport.   It exprefsly fays,
That no petition henceforth fhall be made,
For thirty days, fave only to the king;

Nor

Nor pray'r nor interceffion fhall be heard
Of any God, or man, but of Darius.

DANIEL.

And think'ft thou then my rev'rence for the king,
Good as he is, fhall tempt me to renounce
My fworn allegiance to the King of kings?
Haft thou commanded legions, tempted death
In various fhapes, and fhrink'ft at danger now?
Come, learn of me; I'll teach thee to be bold,
Tho' fword I never drew! Fear not, Arafpes,
The feeble vengeance of a mortal man,
Whofe breath is in his noftrils; for wherein
Is he to be accounted of? but fear
Th' awaken'd vengeance of the living LORD;
He who can plunge the everlafting foul
In infinite perdition!

ARASPES.
Then, O Daniel!
If thou perfift to difobey the edict,
Retire, and hide thee from the prying eyes
Of bufy malice!

DANIEL.
He who is afham'd
To vindicate the honour of his GOD,
Of him the living LORD fhall be afham'd,
When he fhall judge the tribes!

ARASPES.
Yet, O remember,
Oft have I heard thee fay, the fecret heart
Is fair Devotion's Temple; there the faint,

Ev'n

Ev'n on that living altar, lights the flame
Of pureſt ſacrifice, which burns unſeen,
Not unaccepted.—I remember too,
When Syrian Naaman *, by Eliſha's hand,
Was cleans'd from foul pollution, and his mind,
Enlighten'd by the miracle, confeſs'd
The Almighty GOD of Jacob, that he deem'd it
No flagrant violation of his faith,
To bend at Rimmon's ſhrine ; nor did the Seer
Forbid the rite external.

DANIEL.

                              Know, Araſpes,
Heav'n deigns to ſuit our trials to our ſtrength !
A recent convert, feeble in his faith,
Naaman, perhaps, had ſunk beneath the weight
Of ſo ſevere a duty. But ſhall I,
Shall Daniel, ſhall the ſervant of the Lord,
A vet'ran in his cauſe ; one train'd to know,
And do his will; one exercis'd in woe,
Bred in captivity, and born to ſuffer ;
Shall I, from known, from certain duty ſhrink
To ſhun a threaten'd danger ? O, Araſpes !
Shall I, advanc'd in age, in zeal decline ?
Grow careleſs as I reach my journey's end ?
And ſlacken in my pace, the goal in view ?
Periſh diſcretion, when it interferes
With duty ! Periſh the ſafe policy
Of human wit, where GOD's eternal name
Is put in competition ! Shall his law.

                                        Be

Be fet at nought, that I may live at eafe?
How would the heathen triumph, fhould I fall
Thro' coward fear! How wou'd GOD's enemies
Infultingly blafpheme!

ARASPES.
Yet think a moment.

DANIEL.
No!————
Where evil may be *done*, 'tis right to ponder:
Where only *fuffer'd*, know, the fhorteft paufe
Is much too long. Had great Darius paus'd,
This ill had been prevented. But for me,
Arafpes! to deliberate is to fin.

ARASPES.
Think of thy pow'r, thy favour with Darius:
Think of thy life's importance to the tribes,
Scarce yet return'd in fafety. Live! O, live!
To ferve the caufe of Goa!

DANIEL.
GOD will fuftain
Himfelf his righteous caufe. He knows to raife
Fit inftruments to ferve him. As for me,
The fpacious earth holds not a bait to tempt me.
What wou'd it profit me, if I fhou'd gain
Imperial Ecbatan, th' extended land
Of fruitful Media, nay, the world's wide round,
If my eternal foul muft be the price?
Farewell, my friend! time preffes. I have ftol'n
Some moments from my duty, to confirm,
And ftrengthen thy young faith! Let us fulfil
What Heav'n enjoins, and leave to Heav'n th' event!
U   DANIEL.

D A N I E L.

P A R T V.

SCENE, The Palace.

PHARNACES, SORANUS.

PHARNACES.

'TIS done—fuccefs has crown'd our fcheme, Soranus;
And Daniel falls into the deep-laid toils
Our prudence fpread.

SORANUS.
   That he fhou'd fall fo foon,
Aftonifhes ev'n me! What! not a day,
No, not a fingle moment to defer
His rafh devotions? Madly thus to rufh
On certain peril quite tranfcends belief!
When happen'd it, Pharnaces?

        PHAR-

PHARNACES.

                    On the inftant:
Scarce is the deed accomplifh'd.   As he made
His oftentatious pray'r, ev'n in the face
Of the bright God of Day, all Babylon
Beheld the infult offer'd to Darius.
For, as in bold defiance of the law,
His windows were not clos'd.   Our chofen bands,
Whom we had plac'd to note him, ftrait rufh'd in,
And feiz'd him in the warmth of his blind zeal,
Ere half his pray'r was finifh'd.   Young Arafpes,
With all the wild extravagance of grief,
Prays, weeps, and threatens.   Daniel filent ftands,
With patient refignation, and prepares
To follow them.—But fee! the king approaches!

SORANUS.

How's this? deep forrow fits upon his brow!
And ftern refentment fires his angry eye!

DARIUS, PHARNACES, SORANUS.

DARIUS.

O, deep-laid ftratagem! O, artful wile!
To take me unprepar'd! to wound my heart,
Ev'n where it feels moft tenderly, in friendfhip!
To ftab my fame! to hold me up a mark
To future ages, for the perjur'd prince,
Who flew the friend he lov'd! O Daniel! Daniel!
Who now fhall truft Darius? Not a flave
Within my empire, from the Indian main
To the cold Cafpian, but is more at eafe
Than I, his monarch! I have done a deed

                    U 2   Will

Will blot my honour with eternal ftain!
Pharnaces! O, thou hoary fcycophant!
Thou wily politician! thou haft fnar'd
Thy unfufpecting mafter!

PHARNACES.
                              Great Darius!
Let not refentment blind thy royal eyes.
In what am I to blame? who cou'd forefee
This obftinate refiftance to the law?
Who cou'd forefee that Daniel wou'd, perforce,
Oppofe the king's decree?

DARIUS.
                    Thou, thou forefaw'ft it!
Thou knew'ft his righteous foul wou'd ne'er endure
So long an interval of pray'r.   But I,
Deluded king! 'Twas I fhou'd have forefeen
His ftedfaft piety.   I fhou'd have thought,
Your earneft warmth had fome more felfifh fource,.
Something that touch'd you nearer, than your love,.
Your counterfeited zeal for me.——Thou knew'ft
How dear I held him: how I priz'd his truth!
Did I not chufe him from a fubject world,
Unblefs'd by fortune, and by birth ungrac'd,
A captive and a Jew? and yet I lov'd him!
Was he not rich in independent worth?
There, there he fell! If he had been lefs great,
He had been fafe.   Thou cou'dft not bear his brightnefs;
The luftre of his virtues quite obfcur'd,
And dimm'd thy fainter merit. . Rafh old man!
Go, and devife fome means to fet me free
From this dread load of guilt! Go, fet at work

                                                          Thy

Thy plotting genius to redeem the life
Of venerable Daniel!

PHARNACES.

　　　　　　　'Tis too late.
He has offended 'gainſt the new decree;
Has dar'd to make petition to his God,
Altho' the dreadful ſentence of the act
Full well he knew. And by th' eſtabliſh'd law
Of Media, by that law irrevocable,
Which he has dar'd to violate, he dies!

DARIUS.

　　Impiety! preſumption! monſtrous pride!—
Irrevocable? Is there ought on earth
Deſerves that name? Th' eternal laws alone
Of Orofmaſdes claim it. But, alas!
All human projects are ſo faintly fram'd,
So feebly plann'd, ſo liable to change,
So mix'd with error in their very form,
That mutable and mortal are the ſame.
But where is Daniel? Wherefore comes he not
To load me with reproaches? to upbraid me
With all the wrongs my barb'rous haſte has done him!
Where is he?

PHARNACES.

　　　　　　　He prepares to meet his fate.
This hour he dies, for ſo the act decrees.

DARIUS.

　　Suſpend the bloody ſentence! Bring him hither!
Or rather let me ſeek him, and implore
His dying pardon, and his parting pray'r.

DANIEL.

D A N I E L.

P A R T VI.

SCENE, DANIEL's House.

DANIEL ARASPES.

ARASPES.

STILL let me follow thee; still let me hear
The voice of Wisdom, ere the silver cord
By Death's cold hand be loosen'd.

DANIEL.
          Now I'm ready!
No grief; no woman's weakness, good Araspes!
Thou shou'dst rejoice my pilgrimage is o'er;
And the blest haven of repose in view.

ARASPES.

ARASPES.

And muſt I looſe thee, Daniel? muſt thou die?

DANIEL.

And what is death, my friend, that I ſhou'd fear it?
To die! why 'tis to triumph; 'tis to join
The great aſſembly of the good and juſt;
Immortal worthies, heroes, prophets, ſaints!
Oh! 'tis to join the band of holy men,
Made perfect by their ſuff'rings! 'Tis to meet
My great progenitors! 'tis to behold
Th' illuſtrious Patriarchs; they, with whom the Lord
Deign'd hold familiar converſe! 'Tis to ſee
Bleſs'd Noah and his children, once a world!
'Tis to behold (oh! rapture to conceive!)
Thoſe we have known, and lov'd, and loſt, below!
Bold Azariah, and the band of brothers,
Who fought, in bloom of youth, the ſcorching flames!
Nor is it to behold heroic men
Alone, who fought the fight of faith on earth;
But heav'nly conquerors, angelic hoſts,
Michael and his bright legions, who ſubdued
The foes of truth! To join their bleſt employ
Of love and praiſe! To the high melodies
Of choirs celeſtial to attune my voice,
Accordant to the golden harps of ſaints!
To join in bleſs'd hoſannahs to their King!
Whoſe face to ſee, whoſe glory to behold,
Alone were heav'n, tho' ſaint or ſeraph none
There were beſide, and only HE were there!
This is to die! Who wou'd not die for this?
Who wou'd not die, that he might live for ever?

DARIUS.

DARIUS, DANIEL, ARASPES.

DARIUS.

Where is he? Where is Daniel? Let me see him!
Let me embrace that venerable form,
Which I have doom'd to glut the greedy maw
Of furious lions!

DANIEL.
King Darius, hail!

DARIUS.

O, injur'd Daniel! can I see thee thus?
Thus uncomplaining? can I bear to hear
That when the ruffian ministers of death
Stopp'd thy unfinish'd pray'r, thy pious lips
Had just invok'd a blessing on Darius,
On him who sought thy life? Thy murd'rers dropt
Tears of strange pity. Look not on me thus,
With mild benignity! Oh! I could bear
The voice of keen reproach, or the strong flash
Of fierce resentment; but I cannot stand
That touching silence, nor that patient eye
Of meek respect!

DANIEL.
Thou art my master still.

DARIUS.
I am thy murd'rer! I have sign'd thy death!

DANIEL.
I know thy bent of soul is honourable:
Thou hast been gracious still! Had it been otherwise,

I wou'd

I wou'd have met th' appointment of high Heav'n
With humble acquiefcence; but to know,
Thy will concurr'd not with thy fervant's fate,
Adds joy to refignation.

DARIUS.

               Here I fwear,
By him who fits inthron'd in yon bright fun,
Thy blood fhall be aton'd! On thefe, thy foes,
Thou fhalt have ample vengeance.

DANIEL.

               Hold, O king!
Vengeance is mine, th' eternal LORD has faid;
And I will recompence, with even hand,
The finner for the fin. The wrath of man
Works not the righteoufnefs of GOD.

DARIUS.

               I had hop'd
We fhou'd have trod this bufy ftage together,
A little longer; then have funk to reft,
In honourable age! Who now fhall guide
My fhatter'd bark in fafety? who fhall now
Direct me? O, unhappy ftate of kings!
'Tis well the robe of majefty is gay,
Or who wou'd put it on? A crown! what is it?
It is to bear the mis'ries of a people!
To hear their murmurs, feel their difcontents,
And fink beneath a load of fplendid care!
To have your beft fuccefs afcrib'd to Fortune,
And Fortune's failures all afcrib'd to you!

X

It

It is to fit upon a joyleſs height,
To every blaſt of changing fate expos'd !
Too high for hope! too great for happineſs !
For friendſhip too much fear'd! To all the joys
Of ſocial freedom, and th' endearing charm
Of lib'ral interchange of ſoul unknown!
Fate meant me an exception to the reſt,
And, tho' a monarch, bleſs'd me with a friend;
And I—have murder'd him!

DANIEL.

My hour approaches!
Hate not my mem'ry, king, proteĉt Araſpes.
Encourage Cyrus in the holy work
Of building ruin'd Solyma. Farewell!

DARIUS.

With moſt religious ſtriĉtneſs I'll fulfil
Thy laſt requeſt. Araſpes ſhall be next
My throne and heart. Farewell!   [*They embrace.*
Hear, future kings!
Ye unborn rulers of the nations, hear!
Learn from my crime, from my misfortune learn,
Never to truſt to weak, or wicked hands,
That delegated pow'r, which Oromaſdes
Inveils in monarchs for the public good.

DANIEL.

D A N I E L.

P A R T   VII.

S C E N E,   The Court of the Palace.

[The sun rising.

DARIUS, ARASPES.

DARIUS.

OH, good Arafpes! what a night of horror!
To me the dawning day brings no return
Of cheerfulnefs or peace! No balmy fleep
Has feal'd thefe eyes, no nourifhment has paft
Thefe loathing lips, fince Daniel's fate was fign'd!
Hear what my fruitlefs penitence refolves—
The thirty days my rafhnefs had decreed
The edict's force fhou'd laft, I will devote
To mourning and repentance, fafting, pray'r,
And all due rites of grief.   For thirty days,
No pleafant found of dulcimer or harp,
Sackbut, or flute, or pfaltry fhall charm
My ear, now dead to ev'ry note of joy!

X 2

ARASPES.

ARASPES.

My grief can know no period!

DARIUS.

                    See, that den!
There Daniel met the furious lions' rage!
There were the patient martyr's mangled limbs
Torn piece-meal! Never hide thy tears, Araspes;
'Tis virtuous sorrow, unallay'd like mine
By guilt and fell remorse! Let us approach.
Who knows but that dread pow'r, to whom he pray'd
So often and so fervently, has heard him!
                    [*He goes to the mouth of the den.*
O, Daniel, servant of the living GOD!
He whom thou hast serv'd so long, and lov'd so well,
From the devouring lions' famish'd jaw,
Can he deliver thee?

DANIEL. [*From the bottom of the den.*
He can, he has!

DARIUS.

Methought, I heard him speak!

ARASPES.

                    O wond'rous force
Of strong imagination! were thy voice
Loud as the trumpet's blast, it cou'd not wake him
From that eternal sleep!

DANIEL.   [*In the den.*
                    Hail! king Darius!
The God I serve has shut the lion's mouth,
To vindicate my innocence.
                    DARIUS.

DARIUS.
He fpeaks!

He lives!

ARASPES.
'Tis no illufion: 'tis the found
Of his known voice.

DARIUS.
Where are my fervants? hafte,
Fly fwift as light'ning, free him from the den,
Releafe him, bring him hither! Break the feal
Which keeps him from me! See, Arafpes! look!
See the charm'd lions!—Mark their mild demeanor;
Arafpes, mark!—they have no pow'r to hurt him!
See how they hang their heads, and fmooth their fiercenefs,
At his mild afpect!

ARASPES.
Who that fees this fight,
Who that in after-times fhall hear this told,
Can doubt if Daniel's God be God indeed?

DARIUS.
None, none, Arafpes!

ARASPES.
Ah! he comes; he comes!

Enter DANIEL, *followed by multitudes.*

DANIEL.
Hail, great Darius!
DARIUS.

DARIUS.
Doft thou live indeed?
And live unhurt?

ARASPES.
O, miracle of joy!

DARIUS.
I fcarce can truft my eyes! How didft thou 'fcape?

DANIEL.
That bright and glorious Being, who vouchfaf'd
Prefence divine, when the three mar:yr'd brothers
Effay'd the caldron's flame, fupported me!
Ev'n in the furious lions' dreadful den,
The prifoner of hope, even there I turn'd
To the ftrong hold, the bulwark of my ftrength,
Ready to hear, and mighty to redeem!

DARIUS.   [To Arafpes.
Where is Pharnaces! Take the hoary traitor;
Take too Soranus, and the chief abettors
Of this dire edict.   Let not one efcape.
The punifhment their deep-laid hate devis'd
For holy Daniel, on their heads fhall fall
With tenfold vengeance.   To the lions' den
I doom his vile accufers! All their wives,
Their children too, fhall fhare one common fate!
Take care that none efcape.—Go, good Arafpes.

DANIEL.   [Arafpes goes out.
Not fo, Darius.
O fpare the guiltlefs; fpare the guilty too!
Where fin is not, to punifh were unjuft;

And.

And where fin is, O king! there fell remorfe
Supplies the place of punifhment!

DARIUS.

              No more!
My word is paft! Not one requeft, fave this,
Shalt thou e'er make in vain. Approach, my friends,
Arafpes has already fpread the tale,
And fee, what crowds advance.

PEOPLE.

              Long live Darius!
Long live great Daniel too, the people's friend!

DARIUS.

 Draw near, my fubjects. See this holy man!
Death had no pow'r to harm him. Yon fell band
Of famifh'd lions, foften'd at his fight,
Forgot their nature, and grew tame before him.
The mighty GOD protects his fervants thus!
The righteous thus he refcues from the fnare
Of death; while fraud's artificer fhall fall
In the deep gulf his wily arts devife,
To fnare the innocent!

A COURTIER.

           To the fame den
Arafpes bears Pharnaces and his friends;
Fall'n is their infolence! With pray'r's and tears,
And all the meannefs of high-crefted pride,
When adverfe fortune frowns, they beg for life.
Arafpes will not hear. " You heard not me,
He cries, when I for Daniel's life implor'd;

                         His

'His God protected him! fee now, if yours
Will liften to your cries?"

D A R I U S.
Now hear,
'People, and nations! languages and realms!
O'er whom I rule; Peace be within your walls!
That I may banifh from the minds of men
The rafh decree gone out; hear me refolve
To counteraft its force by one more juft.
In ev'ry kingdom of my wide-ftretch'd realm,
From fair Chaldea to the extremeft bound
Of northern Media, be my edict fent,
And this my ftatute known.   My heralds hafte,
And fpread my royal mandate thro' the land,
That all my fubjects bow the ready knee
To Daniel's God—for he alone is Lord.
Let all adore, and tremble at his name,
Who fits in glory unapproachable
Above the heav'ns—above the heav'n of heavens!
His pow'r is everlafting; and his throne,
Founded in equity and truth, fhall laft
Beyond the bounded reign of time and fpace,
Thro' wide eternity! With his right-arm
He faves, and who oppofes? He defends,
And who fhall injure? In the perilous den
He refcued Daniel from the lions' mouth!
His common deeds are wonders, and his works,
One ever-during chain of miracles!

Enter A R A S P E S.

A R A S P E S.
All hail, O king! Darius live for ever!
May all thy foes be as Pharnaces is!

D A R I U S.

DARIUS.

Araſpes, ſpeak?

ARASPES.

O, let me ſpare the tale!—
'Tis full of horror! Dreadful was the ſight!
The hungry lions, greedy for their prey,
Devour'd the wretched princes, ere they reach'd
The bottom of the den.

DARIUS.

Now, now confeſs,
'Twas ſome ſuperior hand reſtrain'd their rage,
And tam'd their furious appetites.

PEOPLE.

'Tis true!
The God of Daniel is a mighty God!
He ſaves, and he deſtroys.

ARASPES.

O, friend! O, Daniel!
No wav'ring doubts can ever more diſturb
My ſettled faith.

DANIEL.

To God be all the glory!

Y

T H E   E N D.

REFLECTIONS

O F

KING HEZEKIAH,

IN HIS SICKNESS.

Set thine houfe in order, for thou fhalt die.
ISAIAH, xxxviii.

WHAT, and no more ?—Is this my foul, faid I,
My whole of being?—Muft I furely die ?
Be robb'd at once of health, of ftrength, of time,
Of youth's fair promife, and of pleafure's prime ?
Shall I no more behold the face of morn,
The cheerful day-light, and the fpring's return ?
Muft I the feftive bow'r, the banquet leave,
For the dull chambers of the darkfome grave ?

Have

Have I confider'd what it is to die ?
In native duft with kindred worms to lie ;
To fleep in cheerlefs cold negleft ; to rot ;
My body loath'd, my very name forgot !
Not one of all thofe parafites, who bend
The fupple knee, their monarch to attend !
What, not one friend ! No, not an hireling flave,
Shall hail GREAT HEZEKIAH in the grave !
Where's he, who falfely claim'd the name of *Great* ?
Whofe eye was terror, and whofe frown was fate ;
Who aw'd an hundred nations from the throne ?
See where he lies, dumb, friendlefs, and alone !
Which grain of duft proclaims the noble birth ?
Which is the royal particle of earth ?
Where are the marks, the princely enfigns where ?
Which is the flave, and which great David's heir ?
Alas ! the beggar's afhes are not known
From his, who lately fat on Ifrael's throne !

How ftands my great account ? My foul, furvey
The debt ETERNAL JUSTICE bids thee pay !
Shou'd I frail Memory's records ftrive to blot,
Will Heav'n's tremendous reck'ning be forgot ?
Can I, alas ! the awful volume tear ?
Or raze one page of the dread regifter ?

" *Prepare thy houfe, thy heart in order fet* ;
" *Prepare, the Judge of Heaven and Earth to meet.*"
So fpake the warning Prophet.—Awful words !
Which fearfully my troubled foul records.
Am I prepar'd ? and *can* I meet my doom,
Nor fhudder at the dreaded wrath to come ?

Y 2

Is

Is all in order fet, my houfe, my heart?
Does no befetting fin ftill claim a part?
Does no one cherifh'd vice, with ling'ring pace,
Reluctant leave me to the work of grace?
Did I each day for this great day prepare,
By righteous deeds, by fin-fubduing pray'r?
Did I each night, each day's offence repent,
And each unholy thought and word lament?
Still have thefe ready hands th' afflicted fed,
And minifter'd to Want her daily bread?
The caufe, I knew not, did I well explore?
Friend, advocate, and parent of the poor?
Did I, to gratify fome fudden guft
Of thoughtlefs appetite; fome impious luft
Of pleafure or of power, fuch fums employ
As wou'd have crown'd pale penury with joy?
Did I in groves forbidden altars raife,
Or molten Gods adore, or idols praife?
Did my firm faith to Heav'n ftill point the way?
Did charity to man my actions fway?
Did meek eye'd Patience all my fteps attend?
Did gen'rous Candour mark me for her friend?
Did I unjuftly feek to build my name
On the pil'd ruins of another's fame?
Did I, like hell, abhor th' infidious lie,
The low deceit, th' unmanly calumny?
Did my fix'd foul the impious wit deteft?
Did my firm virtue fcorn th' unhallow'd jeft;
The fneer profane, and the poor ridicule
Of fhallow Infidelity's dull fchool?
Did I ftill live as born one day to die,
And view th' eternal world with conftant eye?

If fo I liv'd, if fo I kept thy word,
In mercy view, in mercy hear me, LORD!
My holieft deeds *indulgence* will require,
The beft but to *forgivenefs* will afpire;
If thou my pureft fervices regard,
'Twill be with pardon only, not reward!

How imperfection's ftamp'd on all below!
How fin intrudes on all we fay or do!
How late in all the infolence of health,
I charm'd th' Affyrian * by my boaft of wealth!
How fondly, with elab'rate pomp, difplay'd
My glitt'ring treafures! with what triumph laid
My gold and gems before his dazzled eyes,
And found a rich reward in his furprife!
O, mean of foul! can wealth elate the heart,
Which of the man himfelf is not a part?
O, poverty of pride! O, foul difgrace!
Difgufted Reafon, blufhing, hides her face.
Mortal, and proud! ftrange contradicting terms!
Pride for Death's victim, for the prey of worms!
Of all the wonders which th' eventful life
Of man prefents; of all the mental ftrife
Of warring paffions; all the raging fires
Of furious appetites, and mad defires,
Not one fo ftrange appears as this alone,
That man is proud of what is not his own.

How

---

* *This is an anachronifm. Hezekiah did not fhew his treafures to the Affyrian till after his recovery from his ficknefs.*

How fhort is human life! the very breath,
Which frames my words, accelerates my death.
Of this fhort life how large a portion's fled!
To what is gone I am already dead;
As dead to all my years and minutes paft,
As I, to what remains, fhall be at laft.
Can I my cares and pains fo far forget,
To view my vanifh'd years with fond regret?
Can I again my worn-out fancy cheat?
Indulge frefh hope? folicit new deceit?
Of all the vanities weak man admires,
Which greatnefs gives, or fanguine youth defires,.
Of thefe, my foul, which haft thou not enjoy'd?
With each, with all, thy fated pow'rs are cloy'd.
What can I then expect from length of days?
More wealth, more wifdom, pleafure, health, or praife?
More pleafure! hope not that, deluded king?
For when did age increafe of pleafure bring?
Is health, of years prolong'd the common boaft?
And dear-earn'd praife, is it not cheaply loft?
More wifdom! that indeed were happinefs;
That were a wifh a king might well confefs:
But when did Wifdom covet length of days;
Or feek its blifs.in pleafure, wealth, or praife?
No:——Wifdom views with an indifferent eye
All finite joys, all bleffings born to die.
The foul on earth is an immortal.gueft,
Compell'd to ftarve at an unreal feaft:
A fpark, which upward tends by nature's force;
A ftream, diverted from its parent fource;
A drop,. diffever'd from the boundlefs fea;
A moment, parted from. eternity;

A pil-

A pilgrim, panting for the reft to come ?
An exile, anxious for his native home. //

'Why fhou'd I afk my forfeit life to fave ?
Is Heav'n unjuft, which doonis me to the grave ?
Was I with hope of endlefs days deceiv'd ?
Or of lov'd life am I alone bereav'd ?
Let all the great, the rich, the learn'd, the wife,
Let all the fhades of Judah's monarchs rife ;
And fay, if genius, learning, empire, wealth,
Youth, beauty, virtue, ftrength, renown, or health,
Has once revers'd th' immutable decree
On Adam pafs'd, of man's mortality ?
What—have thefe eyes ne'er feen the felon worm
The damafk cheek devour, the finifh'd form ?
On the pale rofe of blafted beauty feed,
And riot on the lip fo lately red ?
Where are our fathers ? Where th' illuftrious line
Of holy prophets, and of men divine ?
Live they for ever ? Do they fhun the grave ?
Or when did Wifdom its profeffor fave ?
When did the brave efcape ? When did the breath
Of Eloquence charm the dull ear of Death ?
When did the cunning argument avail,
The polifh'd period, or the varnifh'd tale;
The eye of lightning, or the foul of fire,
Which thronging thoufands crowded to admire ?
Ev'n while we praife the verfe, the poet dies ;
And filent as his lyre great David lies.
Thou, blefs'd Ifaiah ! who, at God's command,
Now fpeak'ft repentance to a guilty land,

Muft

Muſt die! as wiſe and good thou hadſt not been,
As Nebat's ſon, who taught the land to ſin !

And ſhall I, then, be ſpar'd ? O monſtrous pride!
Shall I eſcape, when Solomon has died ?
If all the worth of all the ſaints was vain—
Peace, peace, my troubled ſoul, nor dare complain !
LORD ! I ſubmit.   Complete thy gracious will !
For if Thou ſlay me *, I will truſt Thee ſtill.
O be my will ſo ſwallow'd up in thine,
That I may do *thy* will in doing *mine.*

---

* *Job.*

T H E   E N D.

SENSIBILITY:

A

POETICAL EPISTLE

TO THE

HON. MRS. BOSCAWEN. *

Spirits are not finely touch'd
But to fine iffues——— SHAKESPEARE.

ACCEPT, BOSCAWEN! thefe unpolifh'd lays,
Nor blame too much the verfe you cannot praife.
For you far other bards have wak'd the ftring;
Far other bards for you were wont to fing.
Yet on the gale their parting mufic fteals,
Yet, your charm'd ear the lov'd impreffion feels.
You heard the lyres of LYTTLETON and YOUNG;
And this a Grace, and that a Seraph ftrung.

Z   Thefe

* * *

* This little Poem was fent feveral years ago, as an
Epiftle, to the honoured Friend to whom it is infcribed. It
has fince been enlarged; and feveral paffages have been
added, or altered, as circumftances required.

Thefe are no more! But not with thefe decline
The Attic chaftenefs, and the flame divine.
Still, *fad * Elfrida's Poet* fhall complain,
And either WARTON breathe his claffic ftrain.
Nor fear left genuine poefy expire,
While tuneful BEATTIE wakes old Spenfer's lyre.
His fympathetic lay his foul reveals,
And paints the perfeÆ *Bard* from what he feels.

　　Illuftrious LOWTH †! for him the mufes wove,
The faireft garland from the greeneft grove.
Tho' Latian bards had gloried in his name,
When in full brightnefs burnt the Latian flame:
Yet, fir'd with nobler hopes than tranfient Bays,
He fcorn'd the meed of perifhable praife;
Spurn'd the cheap wreath by human fcience won,
Borne on the wing fublime of Amos' fon:
He feiz'd his mantle as the Prophet flew,
And with his mantle caught his fpirit too.

　　To fnatch bright beauty from devouring fate,
And bid it boaft with him a deathlefs date;
To fhew how Genius fires, how Tafte reftrains,
While what both are his pencil beft explains,
Have we not REYNOLDS ‡? Lives not JENYNS yet,
To prove his loweft title was a Wit?
Tho' purer flames thy hallow'd zeal infpire
Than e'er were kindled at the Mufe's fire;

Thee,

---

* *Milton calls Euripides——Sad EleÆtra's Poet.*
† *The Bifhop of London.*
‡ *See his Difcourfes to the Academy.*

Thee, mitred * CHESTER! all the Nine shall boast:
And is not JOHNSON theirs, himself an host?

Yes:—still for you your gentle stars dispense
The charm of friendship, and the feast of sense.
Yours is the bliss, and Heav'n no dearer sends,
To call the wisest, brightest, best—your friends.

With CARTER trace the wit to Athens known,
Or find in MONTAGU that wit our own.
Or, pleas'd, attend CHAPONE's instructive page;
Which charms her own, and forms the rising age.
Or boast in WALSINGHAM the various pow'r,
To footh the lonely, grace the letter'd hour;
To polish'd life its highest charm she gives,
Whose fong is music, and whose canvafs lives.
DELANY shines, in worth serenely bright,
Wisdom's strong ray, and Virtue's milder light;
And she who bless'd the friend, and grac'd the page
Of Swift, still lends her lustre to our age:
Long, long protract thy light, O star benign!
Whose setting beams with added brightness shine!

O, much-lov'd BARBAULD! shall my heart refuse
Its tribute to thy Virtues and thy Muse?
While round thy brow the Poet's wreathe I twine,
This humble merit shall at least be mine,
In all thy praise to take a gen'rous part;
Thy laurels bind thee closer to my heart:

Z 2

My

---

* See the Bishop's admirable Poem on Death.

My verfe thy merits to the world fhall teach,
And love the genius it defpairs to reach.

Yet, what is wit, and what the Poet's art?
Can Genius fhield the vulnerable heart?
Ah, no! where bright imagination reigns,
The fine wrought-fpirit feels acuter pains:
Where glow exalted fenfe, and tafte refin'd,
There keener anguifh rankles in the mind:
There feeling is diffus'd thro' ev'ry part,
Thrills in each nerve, and lives in all the heart:
And thofe, whofe gen'rous fouls each tear wou'd keep
From others' eyes, are born themfelves to weep.

Say, can the boafted pow'rs of wit and fong,
Of life one pang remove, one hour prolong?
Prefumptuous hope! which daily truths deride;
For you, alas! have wept—and GARRICK dy'd!
Ne'er fhall my heart his lov'd remembrance lofe,
Guide, critic, guardian, glory of my mufe!
Oh, fhades of Hampton! witnefs as I mourn,
Cou'd wit or fong elude *his* deftin'd urn?
Tho' living virtue ftill your haunts endears,
Yet bury'd worth fhall juftify my tears!
GARRICK! thofe pow'rs which form a friend were thine;
And let me add, with pride, that friend was mine:
With pride! at once the vain emotion's fled;
Far other thoughts are facred to the dead.

Who now with fpirit keen, yet judgment cool,
Th' unequal wand'rings of my mufe fhall rule?
Whofe partial praife my worthlefs verfe enfure?
For Candor fmil'd, when GARRICK wou'd endure.

fI

If harsher critics were compell'd to blame,
I gain'd in friendship what I lost in fame;
And friendship's fost'ring smiles can well repay
What critic rigour justly takes away.
With keen acumen how his piercing eye
The fault, conceal'd from vulgar view, wou'd spy!
While with a gen'rous warmth he strove to hide,
Nay vindicate, the fault his judgment spied.
So pleas'd, cou'd he detect a happy line,
That he wou'd fancy merit ev'n in mine.
Oh gen'rous error, when by friendship bred!
His praises flatter'd me, but not misled.

No narrow views cou'd bound his lib'ral mind;
His friend was man, his party human kind.
Agreed in this, oppofing statesmen strove
Who most shou'd gain his praise, or court his love.
His worth all hearts as to one centre drew;
Thus Tully's Atticus was Cæsar's too.

His wit so keen it never miss'd its end;
So blamelefs too, it never lost a friend;
So chaste, that Modesty ne'er learn'd to fear;
So pure, Religion might unwounded hear.

How his quick mind, strong pow'rs, and ardent heart,
Impoverish'd nature, and exhausted art,
A brighter bard records *, a deathlefs muse!—
But I his talents in his virtues lose:

                                        Great

Great parts are Nature's gift; but that he fhone
Wife, moral, good and virtuous—was his own.
Tho' Time his filent hand acrofs has ftole,
Soft'ning the tints of forrow on the foul;
The deep impreffion long my heart fhall fill,
And every mellow'd trace be perfect ftill.

Forgive, BOSCAWEN, if my forrowing heart,
Intent on grief, forget the rules of art;
Forgive, if wounded recollection melt—
You beft can pardon who have oft'neft felt.
You, who for many a friend and hero mourn,
Who bend in anguifh o'er the frequent urn;
You, who have found how much the feeling heart
Shapes its own wound, and points itfelf the dart;
You, who from tender fad experience feel
The wounds fuch minds receive can never heal;
That grief a thoufand entrances can find,
Where parts fuperior dignify the mind;
Wou'd you renounce the pangs thofe feelings give,
Secure in joylefs apathy to live?

For tho' in fouls, where tafte and fenfe abound,
Pain thro' a thoufand avenues can wound;
Yet the fame avenues are open ftill,
To cafual bleffings as to cafual ill.
Nor is the trembling temper more awake
To every wound which mifery can make,
Than is the finely-fafhion'd nerve alive
To every tranfport pleafure has to give.
For if, when home-felt joys the mind elate,
It mourns in fecret for another's fate;

Yet

Yet when its own fad griefs invade the breaſt,
Abroad, in others bleſſings, fee it bleſt!
Ev'n the ſoft ſorrow of remember'd woe
A not unpleaſing ſadneſs may beſtow.

Let not the vulgar read this penſive ſtrain,
Their jeſts the tender anguiſh wou'd profane:
Yet theſe ſome deem the happieſt of their kind,
Whoſe low enjoyments never reach'd the mind;
Who ne'er a pain but for themſelves have known,
Nor ever felt a ſorrow but their own;
Who call romantic every finer thought,
Conceiv'd by pity, or by friendſhip wrought.
Ah! wherefore happy? where's the kindred mind?
Where, the large ſoul that takes in human kind?
Where, the beſt paſſions of the mortal breaſt?
Where, the warm bleſſing when another's bleſt?
Where, the ſoft lenitives of others' pain,
The ſocial ſympathy, the ſenſe humane?
The ſigh of rapture, and the tear of joy,
Anguiſh that charms, and tranſports that deſtroy?
For tender Sorrow has her pleaſures too;
Pleaſures, which proſp'rous Dulneſs never knew.
She never knew, in all her coarſer bliſs,
The ſacred rapture of a pain like this!
Nor think, the cautious only are the juſt;
Who never was deceiv'd I wou'd not truſt.
Then take, ye happy vulgar! take your part
Of ſordid joy, which never touch'd the heart.
Benevolence, which ſeldom ſtays to chuſe,
Leſt pauſing Prudence teach her to refuſe;
Friendſhip, which once de:ermin'd, never ſwerves,
Weighs ere it truſts, but weighs not ere it ſerves;

And

And foft-ey'd Pity, and Forgivenefs bland,
And melting Charity with open hand;
And artlefs Love, believing and believ'd,
And gen'rous Confidence which ne'er deceiv'd;
And Mercy ftretching out, ere Want can fpeak,
To wipe the tear from pale Affliction's cheek;
Thefe ye have never known!—then take your part
Of fordid joy, which never touch'd the heart.

Ye, who have melted in bright Glory's flame,
Or felt the fpirit-ftirring breath of fame!
Ye noble few! in whom her promis'd meed
Wakes the great thought, and makes the wifh the deed!
Ye, who have tafted the delight to give,
And, God's own agents, bid the wretched live;
Who the chill haunts of Defolation feek,
Raife the funk heart, and flufh the fading cheek!
Ye, who, with penfive Petrarch, love to mourn,
Or weave frefh chaplets for Tibullus' urn;
Who cherifh both in Hammond's plaintive lay,
The Provence myrtle, and the Roman bay!
Ye, who divide the joys, and fhare the pains
Which merit feels, or Heav'n-born Fancy feigns;
Wou'd you renounce fuch joys, fuch pains as thefe,
For vulgar pleafures, or for felfifh eafe?
Wou'd you, to 'fcape the pain the joy forego,
And mifs the tranfport, to avoid the woe?
Wou'd you the fenfe of real forrow lofe,
Or ceafe to woo the melancholy Mufe?
No, Greville *! no!—Thy fong tho' fteep'd in tears,
Tho' all thy foul in all thy ftrain appears;

                                              Yet

---

* See the beautiful Ode to Indifference.

Yet wou'dſt thou all thy well-ſung anguiſh chuſe,
And all th' inglorious peace thou begg'ſt, refuſe.

Or you, BOSCAWEN! when you fondly melt,
In raptures none but mothers ever felt;
And view, enamour'd, in your beauteous race,
All LEVESON's ſweetneſs, and all BEAUFORT's grace!
Yet think what dangers each lov'd child may ſhare,
The youth if valiant, and the maid if fair;
That perils multiply as bleſſings flow,
And conſtant ſorrows on enjoyments grow :
You, who have felt how fugitive is joy,
That while we claſp the phantom we deſtroy;
That life's bright ſun is dimm'd by clouded views,
And who have moſt to love have moſt to loſe;
Yet from theſe fair poſſeſſions wou'd you part,
To ſhield from future pain your guarded heart?
Wou'd your fond mind renounce its tender boaſt,
Or wiſh their op'ning bloom of promiſe loſt?
Yield the dear hopes, which break upon your view,
For all the quiet, Dulneſs ever knew?
Debaſe the objects of your tend'reſt pray'r,
To ſave the dangers of a diſtant care?
Conſent, to ſhun the anxious fears you prove;
They leſs ſhou'd merit, or you leſs ſhou'd love?

Yet, while I hail the Sympathy Divine,
Which makes, O man! the wants of others thine :
I mourn heroic JUSTICE, ſcarcely own'd,
And PRINCIPLE for SENTIMENT dethron'd.
While FEELING boaſts her ever-tearful eye,
Stern TRUTH, firm FAITH, and manly VIRTUE fly.

A a   Sweet

Sweet Sensibility! thou foothing pow'r,
Who fhedd'ft thy bleffings on the natal hour,
Like fairy favours! Art can never feize,
Nor Affectation catch thy pow'r to pleafe:
Thy fubtile effence ftill eludes the chains
Of Definition, and defeats her pains.
Sweet Senfibility! thou keen delight!
Thou hafty moral! fudden fenfe of right!
Thou untaught goodnefs! Virtue's precious feed!
Thou fweet precurfor of the gen'rous deed!
Beauty's quick relifh! Reafon's radiant morn,
Which dawns foft light before Reflexion's born!
To thofe who know thee not, no words can paint!
And thofe who know thee, know all words are faint!
'Tis not to mourn becaufe a fparrow dies;
To rave in artificial extafies:
'Tis not to melt in tender *Otway's* fires;
'Tis not to faint, when injur'd *Shore* expires:
'Tis not becaufe the ready eye o'erflows
At *Clementina's*, or *Clariffa's* woes.

Forgive, O RICHARDSON! nor think I mean,
With cold contempt, to blaft thy peerlefs fcene:
If fome faint love of virtue glow in me,
Pure fpirit! I firft caught that flame from thee.

While foft Compaffion filently relieves,
Loquacious *Feeling* hints how much fhe gives;
Laments how oft her wounded heart has bled,
And boafts of many a tear fhe never fhed.

As words are but th' external marks, to tell
The fair ideas in the mind that dwell;

And

And only are of things the outward fign,
And not the things themfelves, they but define ;
So exclamations, tender tones, fond tears,
And all the graceful drapery Pity wears ;
Thefe are not Pity's felf, they but exprefs
Her inward fufferings by their pictur'd drefs ;
And thefe fair marks, reluctant I relate,
Thefe lovely fymbols may be counterfeit.
Celeftial Pity ! why muft I deplore,
Thy facred image ftamp'd on bafeft ore ?
There are, who fill with brilliant plaints the page,
If a poor linnet meet the gunner's rage :
There are, who for a dying fawn difplay
The tend'reft anguifh in the fweeteft lay ;
Who for a wounded animal deplore,
As if friend, parent, country were no more ;
Who boaft quick rapture trembling in their eye,
If from the fpider's fnare they fave a fly ;
Whofe well-fung forrows every breaft inflame,
And break all hearts but his from whom they came ;
Yet, fcorning life's *dull* duties to attend,
Will perfecute a wife, or wrong a friend ;
Alive to every woe by *fiction* drefs'd ;
The innocent he wrong'd, the wretch diftrefs'd,
May plead in vain ; their fuff'rings come not near,
Or he relieves them cheaply, with a tear.
Not fo the tender moralift * of Tweed ;
His *Man of Feeling* is a man indeed.

A a 2

Oh,

---

* *Mr. Mackenzie, author of the Mirror, Man of Feel-ing, &c.*

Oh, blefs'd Compaffion! Angel Charity!
More dear one genuine deed perform'd for thee,
Than all the periods Feeling e'er can turn,
Than all thy foothing pages, polifh'd STERNE!

Not that by deeds alone this love's expreft,
If fo, the affluent only were the bleft.
One filent wifh, one pray'r, one foothing word,
The precious page of Mercy fhall record;
One foul-felt figh by pow'rlefs Pity giv'n,
Accepted incenfe! fhall afcend to Heav'n.

Since trifles make the fum of human things,
And half our mis'ry from our foibles fprings;
Since life's beft joys confift in peace and eafe,
And few can fave or ferve, but all may pleafe;
Oh! let th' ungentle fpirit learn from hence,
A fmall unkindnefs is a great offence.
Large bounties to beftow we wifh in vain,
But all may fhun the guilt of giving pain.
To blefs mankind with tides of flowing wealth,
With pow'r to grace them, or to crown with health,
Our little lot denies; but Heav'n decrees
To all, the gift of minift'ring to eafe.
The gentle offices of patient love;
Beyond all flatt'ry, and all price above;
The mild forbearance at another's fault,
The taunting word, fupprefs'd as foon as thought;
On thefe Heav'n bade the blifs of life depend,
And crufh'd ill-fortune when he made a FRIEND.

A folitary blefling few can find,
Our joys with thofe we love are intertwin'd;

And

And he, whofe helpful tendernefs removes
Th' obftructing thorn which wounds the breaft he loves,
Smooths not another's rugged path alone,
But fcatters rofes to adorn his own.

The hint malevolent, the look oblique,
The obvious fatire, or implied diflike;
The fneer equivocal, the harfh reply,
And all the cruel language of the eye;
The artful injury, whofe venom'd dart,
Scarce wounds the hearing while it ftabs the heart;
The guarded phrafe whofe meaning kills, yet told,
The lift'ner wonders how you thought it cold;
Small flights, contempt, neglect unmix'd with hate,
Make up in number what they want in weight.
Thefe, and a thoufand griefs minute as thefe,
Corrode our comfort, and deftroy our eafe.

As this ftrong feeling tends to good or ill,
It gives frefh pow'r to vice or principle;
'Tis not peculiar to the wife and good;
'Tis paffion's flame, the virtue of the blood.
But to divert it to its proper courfe,
There Wifdom's pow'r appears, there Reafon's force;
If, ill-directed, it purfues the wrong,
It adds new ftrength to what before was ftrong;
Breaks out in wild irregular defires,
Diforder'd paffions, and illicit fires.
But if the virtuous bias rule the foul,
This lovely feeling then adorns the whole;
Sheds its fweet funfhine on the moral part,
Nor waftes on fancy what fhou'd warm the heart.

Cold

Cold and inert the mental pow'rs would lie,
Without this quick'ning fpark of Deity.
To draw the rich materials from the mine,
To bid the mafs of intellect refine ;
To melt the firm, to animate the cold,
And Heav'n's own imprefs ftamp on nature's gold ; .
To give immortal MIND its fiheft tone,
Oh, SENSIBILITY ! is all thy own.
THIS is th' etherial flame which lights and warms,
In fong tranfports us, and in action charms.
'Tis THIS that makes the penfive ftrains of GRAY *
Win to the open heart their eafy way.
Makes the touch'd fpirit glow with kindred fire,
When fweet SERENA's † poet wakes the lyre.
'Tis THIS, tho' Nature's hidden treafures lie,
Bare to the keen infpection of her eye,
Makes PORTLAND's face its brighteft rapture wear,
When her large bounty fmooths the bed of care.
'Tis THIS that breathes thro' SEVIGNE's fweet page,
That namelefs grace which foothes a fecond age.
'Tis THIS, whofe charms the foul refiftlefs feize,
And gives BOSCAWEN half her pow'r to pleafe.

                                        Yet,

---

* *This is meant of the* Elegy in a Country Church-
yard ; *of which exquifite Poem,* Senfibility *is, perhaps, the
characteriftic beauty.*

† *Triumphs of Temper.*

Yet, why thofe terrors ? why that anxious care,
Since your laft † hope the deathful war will dare ?
Why dread that energy of foul which leads
To dang'rous glory by heroic deeds ?
Why tremble left this ardent foul afpire ?—
You fear the fon becaufe you knew the fire.
Hereditary valour you deplore,
And dread, yet wifh to find one hero more.

---

† *Vifcount Falmouth, Admiral Bofcawen's only remaining fon, was then in America, and at the battle of Lexington.*

F I N I S.

BY THE SAME AUTHOR,

A SEARCH AFTER HAPPINESS,

A DRAMATIC POEM.

PRICE TWO SHILLINGS.